ESCORT PILOT

GUARDING THE AMERICAN BOMBERS OVER WORLD WAR II EUROPE

PHILIP KAPLAN AND ANDY SAUNDERS

Skyhorse Publishing

Skyhorse Publishing books may be purchased in bulk at special discounts for sales promotion, corporate gifts, fund-raising, or educational purposes. Special editions can also be created to specifications. For details, contact the Special Sales Department, Skyhorse Publishing, 307 West 36th Street, 11th Floor, New York, NY 10018 or info@skyhorsepublishing.com.

Skyhorse® and Skyhorse Publishing ® are registered trademarks of Skyhorse Publishing, Inc.®, a Delaware corporation.

Visit our website at www.skyhorsepublishing.com.

10 9 8 7 6 5 4 3 2 1

Library of Congress Cataloging-in-Publication Data is available on file.

Cover design by Rain Saukas
Cover photographs courtesy of Philip Kaplan

Adapted from Little Friends

Print ISBN: 978-1-5107-0512-8
Ebook ISBN: 978-1-5107-0517-3

Printed in China

The cockpit of a newly restored P-51 Mustang escort fighter.

A briefing session of 4th Fighter Group pilots at Debden, Essex, in 1944.

CONTENTS

During World War II he had total control of a 400 mph fighter and eight machine-guns—with no radar, no auto-pilot, and no electronics. At the touch of a button he could unleash thirteen pounds of shot in three seconds. He had a total of fourteen seconds' ammunition. He needed to be less than 250 yards from the enemy to be effective. He and his foe could maneuver in three dimensions at varying speeds and with an infinite number of angles relative to each other. His job was to solve the sighting equation without becoming a target himself. His aircraft carried ninety gallons of fuel between his chest and the engine. He often flew over 35,000 feet with no cockpit heating or pressurization. He endured up to six times the force of gravity with no "G" suit. He had no crash helmet or protective clothing other than ineffective flying boots and gloves. He had about three seconds in which to identify his foe, and slightly longer to abandon the aircraft if hit. He had no ejector seat. He was also a navigator, radio operator, photographer, air-to-ground attacker, rocketeer, and dive-bomber. Often, as in my case, he was only nineteen years old. He was considered too young and irresponsible to vote, but not too young to die. His pay was the modern equivalent of just under sixty new pence per day in 1940. Should he have been stupid enough to be shot down and taken prisoner, a third of that sum was deducted at source by a grateful country and never returned. However, every hour of every day was an unforgettable and marvelous experience shared with some of the finest characters who ever lived.

—Paddy Barthropp, a fighter pilot of the Royal Air Force in World War II

"I want to see you shoot the way you shout."

—Theodore Roosevelt

EVERYTHING ABOUT BRITAIN was strange to the newly arrived Yank. The countryside was greener than anything he had ever seen back home. The weather was lousy and so was the food. The houses looked ancient. The money made no sense to him. The people drove on the wrong side of the road. And when they spoke to him, he couldn't always understand what they said. As Oscar Wilde had put it: "We really have everything in common with America these days except, of course, the language." And there were the shortages, the blackout, the bomb damage, the long lines of shoppers, the crowded trains, the sight of so many men and women in so many different uniforms . . . and the haggard but unbeaten civilians.

The American fighter pilot, however, had made a relatively smooth transition to the UK assignment. First, there had been a trickle of U.S. volunteers into the RAF during the first year of the war in Europe, then a flood of aviators for the Eagle Squadrons preceded the great deluge of airmen arriving late in 1942 to serve with the Eighth and Ninth U.S. Army Air Forces in Britain. With the same mission, and sometimes the same airfields and equipment, the fighter pilots of the USAAF and the RAF were thrown together—living, flying, fighting, and dying alongside each other.

The 31st Fighter Group was the first American fighter unit to be sent to Europe. Its official diarist commented that "operationally we worked direct with the British, which in England was highly efficient—about as good as could ever be attained." It was, for the 31st, a close partnership strengthened by the use of British aircraft on British bases. The 307th Fighter Squadron at Biggin Hill, the 308th at Kenley, and the 309th

Lt. Col. James Clark briefs his 4FG pilots at their Debden base.

The heavily-armed Lockheed P-38 Lightning escort fighter; right: The dogtag identity discs of a Royal Air Force pilot of World War II.

at Westhampnett, all part of the 31st Fighter Group, flew the Spitfire operationally, and the Dieppe raid on August 19, 1942, was their first action. There, Second Lieutenant Samuel Junkin of the 309th shot down a Focke Wulf Fw 190 fighter and became the first USAAF pilot to claim a kill in the European air war. For the first time, pilots of the Eighth Air Force had flown in combat along with fighter pilots of the RAF. That day the American 308th was led into battle over the Dieppe beachhead by RAF Squadron Leader Pete Wickham who had been temporarily detached for the special assignment. Later, the Americans honored him with the Silver Star "for outstanding aerial technique, operational skill, and great courage and determination." From July to October 1944, Wickham he was attached to another U.S. fighter group where he again served with distinction, at North Weald, northeast of London, the same base from which he had led No 111 Squadron, RAF. Another 111 Squadron pilot, George Heighington, had good reason to remember the American fliers with appreciation. On June 2, 1942, the North Weald wing was to be sent on a sweep of the Cap Gris Nez area, but recent losses had reduced the number of available aircraft. To make up for the shortfall, 111 Squadron borrowed a Spitfire from 350 Squadron and assigned it to Heighington.

"It had been a last-minute arrangement and I only went to collect the aircraft as we were due to taxi out for takeoff, so had little or no time to set it up for my own use. During the flight out I set the seat for my own height, adjusted the rudder pedals, and set the throttle quadrant the way I wanted it. Then, as soon as we got over France, we were jumped by a whole hell of a lot of ME 109s and

I switched on my gunsight ready to do battle. Nothing! It just didn't light up. Now this was not a good time to discover you had a malfunction in your gunsight, but I did my best. This turned out to be quite inadequate and I was immediately shot to pieces. As my logbook records: 'Cannon shells in wing and fuselage. Port cannon shot away. Starboard magazine exploded blowing away wing plates. Plates blown from port wing and tail unit. Engine misfiring.' I was virtually dead in the air, just sitting at thirty thousand feet over Dunkirk and at the mercy of the next Luftwaffe pilot to spot me. Then, salvation. Another Spitfire arrived and escorted me back to England in a gentle dive, my engine eventually dying on me before I made a successful dead-stick landing at Manston—severely shaken and lucky to be alive. The pilot who saved me never identified himself, but after I

made a lot of inquiries he turned out to be a member of one of the Eagle Squadrons, Number 133. I'd like to know exactly who he was so I could write him my much-belated thanks. That Yank saved my life."

In addition to Spitfires, Hurricanes were flown by American pilots in the Eagle Squadrons. Carroll McColpin, a former Eagle pilot, preferred them. When he was transferred to a Spitfire unit he felt he had been downgraded. "The Hurricane was a beautiful-flying airplane. If you kept your eyes open nobody could shoot you down in one of those. As long as you could see them they couldn't get you. And it could out-maneuver a Spitfire. Easily. But it was slower on altitude capabilities and with a slower dive. A good old bird it was, with a hell of a lot of firepower. Rugged too. I liked the four sets of controls to your elevators, rudders, and stuff. That meant you could

get shot up on one side and still have control. I liked it a lot."

Conversely, the American P-51 Mustang fighter was used extensively by the RAF. It ultimately proved to be the outstanding fighter of the war and certainly the best escort fighter. The RAF quickly discovered the Mustang's potential and was, by VE Day, operating more than 320 of the planes. The Mustang was a type that had proved its worth in a variety of roles. RAF pilots flying Mustangs escorted British bombers that were attacking German shipping off the Norwegian coast in mid-1944. In addition to the RAF, on August 8, 1944, the famous 4th Fighter Group of the Eighth USAAF, flew escort cover for the RAF bombers off Norway. The Mustang pilots of the 4th took on the assignment when the British Mustangs were shifted to southern England to deal with the threat of the German V-1 flying bombs. For the Americans the flight to Norway was about 800 miles. It was at low level all the way across the North Sea. In addition to the hazard of salt spray, if a pilot went into water that cold, his survival time was measured in minutes. One of the participating RAF bomber pilots recalled his feelings for his American escorts: "They were splendidly and magnificently heroic."

In general, the British and American fighter pilots got along well; there was, however, some friction. The Yanks were, on occasion, accused of being "overpaid, overfed, oversexed, and over here." The Americans countered that the Brits were "underpaid, undersexed, and under Eisenhower." And they grumbled about the food. One American fighter pilot swore that "the British subsisted on some of the most appalling food known to man or beast. Have you ever tried biting on a kipper for breakfast? Worse

still, have you had these things they call Brussels sprouts? If I ever have to crash my plane I'll make sure I do it on a Brussels sprout field."

Living conditions varied greatly in both the American and British air forces. Established prewar bases like Debden, Tangmere, Digby, North Weald, and Martlesham Heath had permanent, brick-built accommodation, central heating, and comfortable furnishings. Those less fortunate airmen assigned to one of the hundreds of muddy bases built during the war could expect only squalid shacks, leaky tin Nissen huts or drafty Maycrete buildings. Keeping warm and dry was a constant struggle. The pot-bellied stoves provided put out as much smoke as they did heat. Some of the pilots had to live in canvas tents, especially those operating from the "advanced landing grounds" near the south coast of England around D-Day.

A pilot of the 31st Fighter Group, U.S. Army Air Force: "Here we were, Johnny-come-latelys to these Limeys who had taken it on the chin for so long. France . . . Dunkirk . . . the Battle of Britain . . . then the Blitz. They'd been there and they had done it. They sure had the edge on us when it came to experience and we knew it. Respected it. What did we have to offer? That's how some of us felt in the beginning. Inadequate. But never once did these RAF types act superior to us freshmen. They welcomed us as equals . . . and that was the key to our getting along, so far as we in the 31st were concerned. At this stage in the air war we knew we weren't equals to our battle-hardened pals . . . but we sure were determined to be! At first they might have had their doubts, but as true English gentlemen they hid them well. Their attitude, and our approach, made for a wonderful partnership. Sure, we were different.

The way we did things, even the way we spoke. But the record of the fighter pilots of the Eighth and Ninth Air Forces speaks for itself, and the RAF guys had blazed a trail for us to follow. We did so with pride and we did it well. The truth is, we couldn't have done it without each other."

She's the girl that makes the thing
That drills the hole, that holds the spring / That drives the rod, that turns the knob / That works the thing-ummybob. / It's a ticklish sort of job Making a thing for a thingummybob Especially when you don't know what it's for. / And it's the girl that makes the thing / That holds the oil that oils the ring / That makes the thingummy-bob that's going to win the war . . .
—anonymous

The walk to headquarters, occasionally asking directions, was enlightening. There was a base hospital, the Red Cross Club for enlisted men, tennis courts, volley ball courts, armament building, movie house, post exchange, photography shop, enlisted men's barracks, and, finally, headquarters. The streets and sidewalks were paved and the grass was carefully cut. In back of all this, three huge hangars loomed, and everything was painted with the characteristic camouflage. Fifteen-hundred officers and men lived on this base, all slaves to the forty-eight P47s sitting around the field. This was Debden.
—from *The Look of Eagles* by John T. Godfrey

The Ops Room state board of the 65th Fighter Wing near Saffron Walden.

When a man wants to murder a tiger, he calls it sport; when the tiger wants to murder him he calls it ferocity.
—George Bernard Shaw from *Maxims for Revolutionists*

WALTER J. KONANTZ FLEW MUSTANGS with the 338th Fighter Squadron, 55th Fighter Group, at Wormingford, England in the Second World War. This was a typical mission day as he remembered it.

0500 hours. The door bursts open in our twelve-man Nissen hut and the CQ flips on the lights and wakes everybody up. A few of the pilots aren't flying today and they can go back to sleep. Those who are flying get dressed and go to the central latrine to brush their teeth and shave.

0530 hours. A big GI truck picks us up and takes us to the mess hall, where we have the usual breakfast of powdered eggs, greasy bacon, burned toast and black coffee. The mess hall is close enough to the briefing room that we all walk over there as each finishes his last cup of coffee.

0615 hours. We find our designated seats in the briefing room. A flight leader sits in the front row with his wing man (number two) immediately behind him. The number three man (element leader) sits behind number two, and directly behind him sits the number four man (tail-end Charlie). The briefing officer can then tell at a glance if anyone is missing and in what position in the formation they are flying. The big map on the wall behind the briefing officer has a red string from our base to the rendezvous point, then to the bombers' target. Zigs and zags in the string show the turning points to help us avoid known flak concentrations. The target for

A beautifully restored North American P-51D Mustang escort fighter.

today is Berlin, which is a five-and-a-half hour mission for us, and over eight hours for the bombers. We are given our engine start times, bomber-rendezvous time and target time. Flak locations are covered, expected enemy opposition is discussed, and the weather for launch, en route, target area, and recovery time is briefed. All pilots hack their GI wristwatches to the exact time and the briefing is concluded. We then check out our parachutes, zip on the anti-G suit, put on a heavy jacket, don the Mae West life vest; heavy gloves and fur-lined boots complete the suiting-up. The cockpit heater in the P-51 only works when the outside air temperature is warm enough that you don't need it anyway. On the way out of the briefing room, they have several boxes of candy bars for "in-flight lunches" and I grab a couple of bars. We gather outside the briefing room, where we are picked up by several GI trucks and hauled to the various dispersal areas where our planes are parked. On arrival at my parking area, my crew

left: World War II Nissen huts at the former Steeple Morden base near Cambridge, England in the 1990s; right: The 355th Fighter Group memorial at Steeple Morden.

chief takes my parachute and places it in the cockpit. I ask him if all the fuel tanks, including the two pressed-paper 110-gallon external tanks, are topped off. He assures me they are full and, trusting him implicitly, I don't bother to check them. He is now standing on the wing helping me buckle into the 'chute and seat harness. He climbs down and stands by the nose of the plane with a fire extinguisher at his side to monitor the engine start.

0730 hours. Some of the planes are starting up and beginning to move, but my start-engine time (written on the back of my hand) is still ten minutes away.

0740 hours. It is time to start my engine. I flip the master switch on, hold the spring-loaded primer switch a few seconds, turn on the ignition switches, and hold the starter switch. The prop blades turn a couple of revolutions and the Merlin engine catches with a few pops and bangs, then roars to life with some puffs of black smoke.

I let it warm up a couple of minutes, signal the crew chief to pull the wheel chocks, and taxi to the line of planes waiting at the hardstand exit to get on the taxiway. I have also written on the back of my hand the identification code letters of the airplane I am to follow and, when he passes by on the taxiway, I pull out behind him. There is a long string of idling P-51s on the taxiway leading to the takeoff end of the runway. There are forty-eight fighters flying this mission, three squadrons of four flights, each flight

An Eighth Air Force attack on an oil refinery near Hamburg, Germany, in 1943.

consisting of four planes. There are also two spares cranked up who will fly to the German border in case they are needed to fill in for an air abort. If they are not needed, they will return to home base. While waiting in the takeoff line, I recheck all my engine instruments, crank in five degrees of right rudder trim (the engine torque is terrific at low speeds and high power), lower the flaps ten degrees for the heavy takeoff weight and check my fuel selector valve on left main.

0800 hours. I taxi onto the runway behind two or three airplanes waiting to take off. I am leading Acorn Blue flight today, so I line up on the left side of the runway and my wingman lines up on the right side. Up ahead is a pilot standing by the left side of the runway with an orange and white checkered flag. He flags off each pair of airplanes when he sees that the preceding pair has cleared the ground. The pair ahead of us is on the take-off roll, so I move up even with the flag man, hold the brakes, and rev up to about twenty-five percent power. The flag man waves the flag over his head in a circular motion to rev up, then drops it to signal brake release. As soon as we start moving, I slowly advance power to sixty-seven inches of manifold pressure and 3,000 rpm. My wingman does the same and we take off together in close formation. As soon as we clear the ground, I signal for landing gear up and, when reaching 140 mph, I signal for flaps up. I can still see two planes ahead of me; the others have disappeared into the one-thousand-foot overcast. I watch the two planes ahead enter the overcast, note their heading, then set my climb course a few degrees to the right of theirs so my wingman and I won't be running into their prop wash while on instruments. The overcast

is only 5,000 feet thick and we break out in bright sunlight at 6,000 feet. Most of the other P-51s are in sight now and we begin closing up with the others into the briefed formation.

0830 hours. All forty-eight Mustangs are in formation, with the two spares following the last flight of four. We are now climbing through to 18,000 feet over the North Sea. I switch the fuel selector to the eighty-five-gallon aft fuselage tank to burn it down to forty gallons to ease the tail-heavy condition before switching to the external drop tanks. My wingman, Acorn Blue Two, is about two hundred feet to my left and fifty feet back. His wingman, Acorn Blue Four, is another two hundred feet out and fifty feet in back of Blue Three. This spreadout battle formation allows the pilots to look around for enemy aircraft without the total concentration required in close-formation flying.

0900 hours. We approach the long stream of eastbound bombers. It is so long that we cannot see the lead B-17s nor the tail end of the stream. We are nearing our rendezvous time and point. Acorn Red Two was elected (as are all of the greenest pilots on their first few missions) to leave our formation, slide up to the side of the bombers and slowly rock his wings while never pointing his nose at them so as not to be mistaken for an ME 109. His job is to get close enough to the bombers to read the symbols on the vertical tail surfaces to see if they are the ones we are assigned to escort. When our bombers are found and identified, our squadron leader puts two flights on either side and two or three thousand feet higher than the B-17s. Our other two squadrons do the same things with their box of bombers farther up the line. I

American 1,000-pound bombs ready to be transported to waiting B-17s and delivered to a target in Germany.

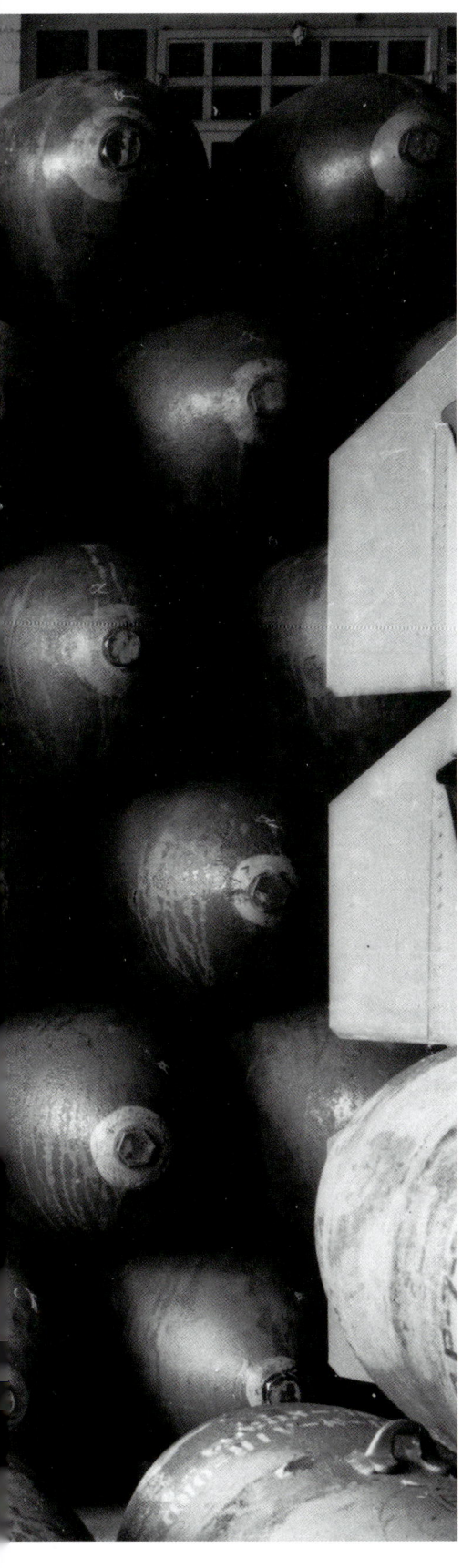

have switched the fuel selector to the left external tank. I will try to run each external tank fifteen minutes before switching to the other one to keep them evenly balanced.

0935 hours. We are crossing the border into Germany now, still climbing through 29,000 feet, and all the planes, bombers and fighters alike, are leaving long vapor trails through the sky. These are caused by the moisture in the engine exhaust freezing instantly when it is ejected into the thirty-degree-below-zero outside air. I switch to the right drop tank as my plane is getting slightly right-wing heavy.

1000 hours. Some fighters farther up the stream report sighting some FW 190s, but we don't see any.

1030 hours. Our bombers are turning onto their final bomb run, heading toward Berlin, and have not yet been under attack by German fighters. As the bombers head in on their bomb run, we back off some distance from them as we see no need for us to share the murderous flak barrage they are getting. The sky around them is black with 88mm flak bursts. I see one B-17 receive a direct hit that explodes his bombs in a massive ball of black smoke and flames. The only recognizable pieces are his four engines falling from the fireball. A minute later, another B-17 slants out of his formation with his left engines and wing on fire. Many B-17s are straggling behind with one or two engines shut down. The weather over Berlin is clear and we can see the flashes of the exploding bombs all over the center of the city. Two more smoke-trailing B-17s leave their formation and head down. I catch a quick glimpse of some of the Fortress crews bailing out, but have

no time to count them to see if they all got out.

1135 hours. We move back over our home-bound bombers and escort them to the Holland border. Since we did not have to drop our external tanks early in anticipation of a dogfight, we have enough fuel to do a little strafing on the way home. I exhausted my drop tanks a short time ago and dropped them from 25,000 feet over an unknown German town, hoping they might do some damage. Acorn Blue flight goes down to 5,000 feet, searching for something to strafe. We soon find a freight train puffing along and in a short time it is riddled wreckage, the engine is spurting steam in all directions.

1150 hours. Acorn Blue flight is headed home but we stay at 5,000 feet still looking for more targets of opportunity. I spot three ME 109s cruising along at our altitude on a crossing path some distance ahead of us. We swing in behind them and go to full power in a stern chase. They see us now and they go to full power, evidenced by the thin streams of black smoke coming from their exhaust stacks. We slowly close on them and, when in range, I open fire on the leader. He is carrying a single external tank under his belly and my armor-piercing incendiary bullets set it afire. He drops the flaming tank and dives toward the ground as the other two 109s break in opposite directions. I press on with the leader and, after some more hits, he bellies in at 250 mph in a snow-covered field, sliding to a stop in a grove of trees. As I pass over the wreckage, the pilot is climbing out and waving at me. Acorn Blue Three gets one of the other ME 109s and Acorn Blue Four gets the last one.

A Mustang escort fighter restoration performing in an air show at Duxford, England. In late 1943, Eighth Air Force heavy bomber losses to enemy fighter attacks were proving unsustainable and were crippling the daylight bombing offensive. The arrival in quantity of the P-51 Mustang with the fighter groups of the Eighth enabled the bomber crews to fly their missions with a much greater chance of survival against the savage attacks of the German Air Force.

1220 hours. Our fuel supply forces us homeward and we climb to 15,000 feet to be safe from light ground fire in Nazi-occupied Holland. As we approach the North Sea, we see two B-17s limping along on three engines and escort them across the water.

1300 hours. We are nearing England now and wave good-bye to the two crippled bombers. I take off my oxygen mask and light a cigarette, then I eat my two "inflight lunch" candy bars. This is my first opportunity to take off the oxygen mask on the mission.

1330 hours. Acorn Blue flight is in a tight echelon-right formation a mile out from the runway at 250 mph and thirty feet off the ground. When we come to the runway, we reduce power, fan upward in a tight lefthand climbing turn, then lower the flaps and landing gear. Each pilot fans upward a second later than the man in front of him so that all four planes are evenly spaced for individual landings. None of us has more than fifteen gallons of fuel left, but the weather is clear and we could have landed at any number of closer RAF or U.S. bases had our fuel supply been really tight.
We have to forego our "victory rolls" over the runway, though, due to our low fuel state.

1340 hours. As I taxi into my circular hardstand, my crew chief notices the tape missing from my gun muzzles and leaps up on the wing. He wants to know what I had shot at. He has another swastika painted on the plane before nightfall. A few minutes after I arrive at the hardstand, a GI truck pulls up and we climb in the back with several other pilots and head for mission debriefing. The flight surgeon is standing at the door of the debriefing room, pouring us

each a shot of "mission whiskey." We get this before the debriefing, I suppose, to relax us and make us more talkative. The intelligence officer debriefs each flight (four pilots at a time), and any member can interrupt and add to what others say. We are queried on what we saw, where we saw it, what time we saw it, and where it was headed. We are asked how many bombers we saw go down, enemy aircraft sighted, how many, etc. Three of us have to fill out separate encounter reports on the three ME 109s we have claimed as destroyed. From the debriefing room we walk a short distance to our squadron operations building to check the mission board to see who is scheduled to fly again tomorrow. We also run the previous day's gun camera film, which is all spliced together on one reel.

1500 hours. GI trucks begin running pilots back to the barracks where most will sack out until suppertime.

1730 hours. Shuttle trucks come by every ten minutes for the next hour to take us to the mess hall. This meal is usually better than the monotonous breakfast. We occasionally have steak or other meat. After the evening meal, many go to the nearby Officers' Club for a few drinks and merrymaking, but I hop a truck back to the barracks with a sack of steak scraps for Lassie, my Scottie dog who lives in the barracks with me. I have a bottle of scotch in my foot locker and those barracks mates who are here don't miss too much by not going to the Club.

2130 hours. The dog has been fed and those pilots flying tomorrow put their drinking cups away and think about going to bed.

Another lovingly restored P-51D Mustang about to touchdown at Duxford airfield after performing in the world-famous Flying Legends annual air show.

2140 hours. The base loudspeaker system announces: "This station is under Red Alert. Seek shelter." The message is repeated a couple of times. This is the signal for us to load our GI .45 caliber pistols and run outside. Our base is right in line with London, so the V-1 buzz bombs launched from HE 111 aircraft over the North Sea pass over us en route. We stand on top of the bomb shelter, pistols in hand, waiting for a buzz bomb to go over. They are usually only a few hundred feet high and can easily be seen at night by the plume of fire from the ram jet engine. The distinctive noise is also a help in locating them. If one comes over, pistol shots from several bomb shelters can be heard. No one has ever hit one as far as we know. One comes over at about two a.m. but no one gets up to seek shelter or to shoot at it. The rumble gets louder, then the engine quits. It is so close we can hear it whistling as it glides. Too late now to seek shelter. I just pull the covers up over my head and wait. Soon there is a thunderous blast that blows open the barracks doors. It has exploded less than a mile away. We close the barracks doors and everyone tries to get back to sleep. There are only three more hours until wake-up time.

0500 hours. The barracks door bursts open, the CQ flips on the lights and . . .

THEY WERE THE TOOLS for the job. Like the pilots who flew them, the fighter aircraft of the Second World War represented high performance and deadly intent. Their splendid nicknames—Mustang, Spitfire, Hurricane, Lightning, Thunderbolt, and Typhoon—implied the great speed, power, and agility of these special warplanes; the state-of-the-art machines designed and built for a brief but efficient life as hunter-killers.

No combat plane is perfect in all respects and knowing an aircraft's limitations is as fundamental to combat survivability as is knowing its capabilities. The most serious limitation of the P-47 Thunderbolt was its comparatively slow rate of climb. It was, though, a remarkably rugged airplane. Armed with a wing-mounted battery of eight .50 caliber Browning machine guns, it could carry underwing rockets and bombs to add to its firepower and destructive capability for the ground-attack role. It was the biggest single-seat, single-engine Allied fighter of the war, and its shape earned it the additional nickname Jug. With its bulbous front and tapering fuselage, it certainly resembled a milk jug.

If the Thunderbolt didn't climb very well, it could surely dive. Its pilots attributed this characteristic to what they called the "milk-bottle effect." Gravity and the massive Pratt & Whitney 2800 Wasp engine driving a huge four-blade propeller made its dive impressive by any standard. Its great size, though, made the first impression on pilots new to the P-47. "Gee," said one Spitfire veteran as he peered into a Thunderbolt cockpit for the first time, "you could walk around in there!"

The Thunderbolt was more than just big. It was an ace maker. In it many Eighth and Ninth Air Force pilots achieved that status. It was the airplane with which the high-achieving 4th and 56th Fighter Groups

first became famous. Once the early engine and radio problems common to the aircraft were overcome, the Thunderbolt became an outstanding fighter—appreciated by its pilots and respected by the Luftwaffe.

In the early 1990s a magnificently restored P-47 was still flown regularly by Stephen Grey of The Fighter Collection, Duxford Airfield, England. "Settle into the cockpit and space plus comfort prevail. Start the 2800 engine and it begins to feel like a 'class act.' Taxi to the hold and it feels like a beautifully damped Mack truck. At run-up it purrs rather than barks. Put the hammer down for takeoff and there is no kick in the back or dart for the weeds. It runs straight and true—if sedately.

"Put the wheels in the wings and it turns into a crisp-handling fighter, with beautiful ailerons, outstanding controls, great visibility, and a sensation of pedigree.

"True, it does not climb with the best of them, but stuff the nose toward the greenery and the airspeed indicator will wind to the stop and stay there faster than any other prop fighters that I have flown. Circuit work, landing, and ground handling are docile and beautifully mannered.

"Fortunately, or regrettably, I have not had to fight in the big Jug. However, from a little 'arm wrestling' with others behind the hangar I know that the Jug could fight incredibly well, if differently. If I were able to transpose myself back to the forties and had a choice, I feel my survival instincts would tell me to choose the big Jug, but my competitive instincts would tell me only to fight on my terms with a lot of airspace underneath me.

"The sheer rugged, technical quality of the airplane is its charm, the handling a joy. When I climb out and walk away, I always find myself looking back at the 47 with affection . . . what a character."

Until the arrival of the P-51 Mustang in the European Theater of Operations, the Republic P-47 Thunderbolt was the dominant Allied escort fighter of the Eighth and Ninth U.S. Army Air Forces.

The Typhoon was the RAF's Thunderbolt. While not quite as big, it was still very large and could deliver equally heavy punishment. But it never achieved the same degree of success. Only one Typhoon of the 3,317 built survives and this is a non-airworthy example in the RAF Museum at Hendon near London.

Above 15,000 feet, the Typhoon's performance could not match that of the Spitfire, the aircraft it was intended to replace. There were problems with its Napier Sabre engine and, more seriously, there were airframe structural failures. But the Typhoon is remembered fondly by many who flew it. One was Jimmy Kyle who, as a twenty-year-old, was a member of No 197 Squadron. "I first flew the Typhoon Mark 1A, with the car door-type hood on 20th December 1942, nine months after it had entered service with the Royal Air Force. The pilot sat high in this big fighter. I stepped in and settled on the hard dinghy base attached to the parachute, which fitted into the bucket seat of the cockpit. I strapped in, clipped on the face mask, plugged in the RT, and switched on the oxy-

gen. With its long nose, three prominent propeller blades, thick anhedral / dihedral wing, wide undercarriage, and four evenly-spaced cannons, the Typhoon conveyed an impression of power and brute strength.

"When settled and feeling at ease, I started the engine with a bang. It could be temperamental. The twenty-four cylinder Napier Sabre was provided with a Coffman starter used in conjunction with a Kigas primer. The amount of priming required depended on the engine temperature and it was imperative to get the combination right for the engine to start without delay. When the starter switch was thrown the engine would spring to life with a loud explosion, causing clouds of acrid exhaust smoke to stream from both sides of the cowling. The smoke quickly thinned and disappeared as the engine warmed up with an even roar.

"I spent a few minutes checking temperatures and pressures. Noting all was well, re-tightening the primer, I waved 'chocks away' to the ground crew, released the brakes, rolled forward, checking that the brakes operated, and taxied slowly out for takeoff.

A wonderful warbird restoration, *No Guts-No Glory!*, a P-47 Thunderbolt of The Fighter Collection, Duxford, England, for many years.

"Tense and excited, cautiously edging forward, I waited for takeoff clearance and swung the nose into the wind and lined the plane up onto the runway . . . positioning it dead center, completing the cockpit checks and revving the engine to clear it. I held hard on the brakes, then slowly released them and gradually opened the throttle to maximum takeoff power. As the stick was pushed forward and the tail unit lifted, there was an unpleasant tendency for the aircraft to swing to starboard. This inherent swing could lead to eventual loss of control if application of the port rudder wasn't anticipated. Being aware of this inbuilt idiosyncrasy I gently fed in a fraction of port rudder slightly before the tail unit was fully up, to prevent the swing.

"The engine surged to a roar as the Typhoon hurtled down the runway. I checked all instruments, eased the control column back and was airborne. Climbing out I was surprised at the ease of the takeoff. Selecting wheels-up and the small amount of flap I used to offset undercarriage strain on the bumpy runway, I noted the green lights go on and then out, indicating undercarriage up, and settled the aircraft in the climb at the recommended speed of about 300 mph. The feeling of power and speed was marvelous. I quickly found myself at a high altitude and leveling out. I then put the aircraft and myself to our respective limits.

"I completed a sequence of aerobatics, stalls, slow rolls, loops, upward rolls, incipient spins, and some barrel rolls on the way down. All the maneuvers were easy to perform but I sustained high G loads that I had not experienced before. The thrust of Gs pushed my sagging jaw and chin down to my chest, and the centrifugal forces drove my blood from my brain into my boots, my vision graying and my legs feeling

like lead. By easing the controls, I could in seconds return to the normal if and when it became too hard to bear.

"On returning to the circuit and slowing to a landing configuration, I carried out a normal continuous curved approach with wheels down and locked. Then, with full flap selected, I turned onto short final—a normal fighter approach, only this one being a little faster than most other aircraft at the time. The ground rushed up quickly. The approach speed in the turn was between 120 and 130 mph, gradually reducing to 95, and further still when rounding out for touchdown at 75 mph.

"I landed safely and, quickly completing the after-landing checks without stopping, taxied back to the dispersal, exhilarated and pleased with the thirty-minute flight. Stepping from the cockpit I jumped to the ground among eager faces awaiting my arrival. All were anxiously awaiting their turn to fly the Typhoon. 'How did it go?' they asked. 'Marvelous,' I said, explaining every detail of the trip to those around me. I then signed the authorization book, 'DCO.' Duty Carried Out.' "

Jimmy Kyle survived his tour on Typhoons and the Typhoons survived their early mechanical and structural problems. An increased frequency of low-altitude German attacks on British coastal towns allowed the Typhoon to establish itself as a premier low-level interceptor. It would later excel as the Allies' key ground-attack aircraft for the RAF's 2nd Tactical Air Force.

Of all the fighter aircraft of the Second World War, the North American P-51 Mustang was simply the best of the Allied examples. This exceptional airplane employed an American airframe and a British engine to achieve its remarkable success. Initially developed

using an Allison engine, it was designated Mustang I when first received by the RAF. Rolls-Royce test pilot Ronnie Harker flew the Mustang I at Duxford in a brief test flight and was impressed. He recognized the potential of the airplane, noting in his report: "The aircraft should prove itself a formidable low and mid-altitude fighter . . . with a powerful and good engine like the Merlin 61 its performance should be outstanding." Harker knew that he was onto something very special in the Mustang—something with great potential. The U.S. Army Air Corps was, however, initially reluctant to abandon its reliance on air-cooled engines in favor of the liquid-cooled Merlin for one of its fighters. But it would have no cause to regret the change, as the Mustang was to become the most formidable fighter in its inventory.

Mustang pilot Robin Olds recalled: "Here was a fighter. High or low. Straight down or in a shuddering Lufberry, you knew no one could match you. The gyro sight was deadly accurate, the firepower devastating. Gun-camera results were like Hollywood, a far cry from the blurred, jumpy imagery produced by the gun-camera in the P-38, where some knothead had mounted the camera right under a 20mm cannon.

"As for actual combat performance, the P-51 was good at everything, more than matching German machines in what they could do. In all, it was a fighter pilot's dream. Just ask any pilot who ever strapped a Mustang to his bottom and set out across the North Sea to do battle with the wily Hun."

Certainly among the greatest contributions of the USAAF to victory in Europe was the part played by its fighters in achieving and maintaining air superiority. The Mustang played a

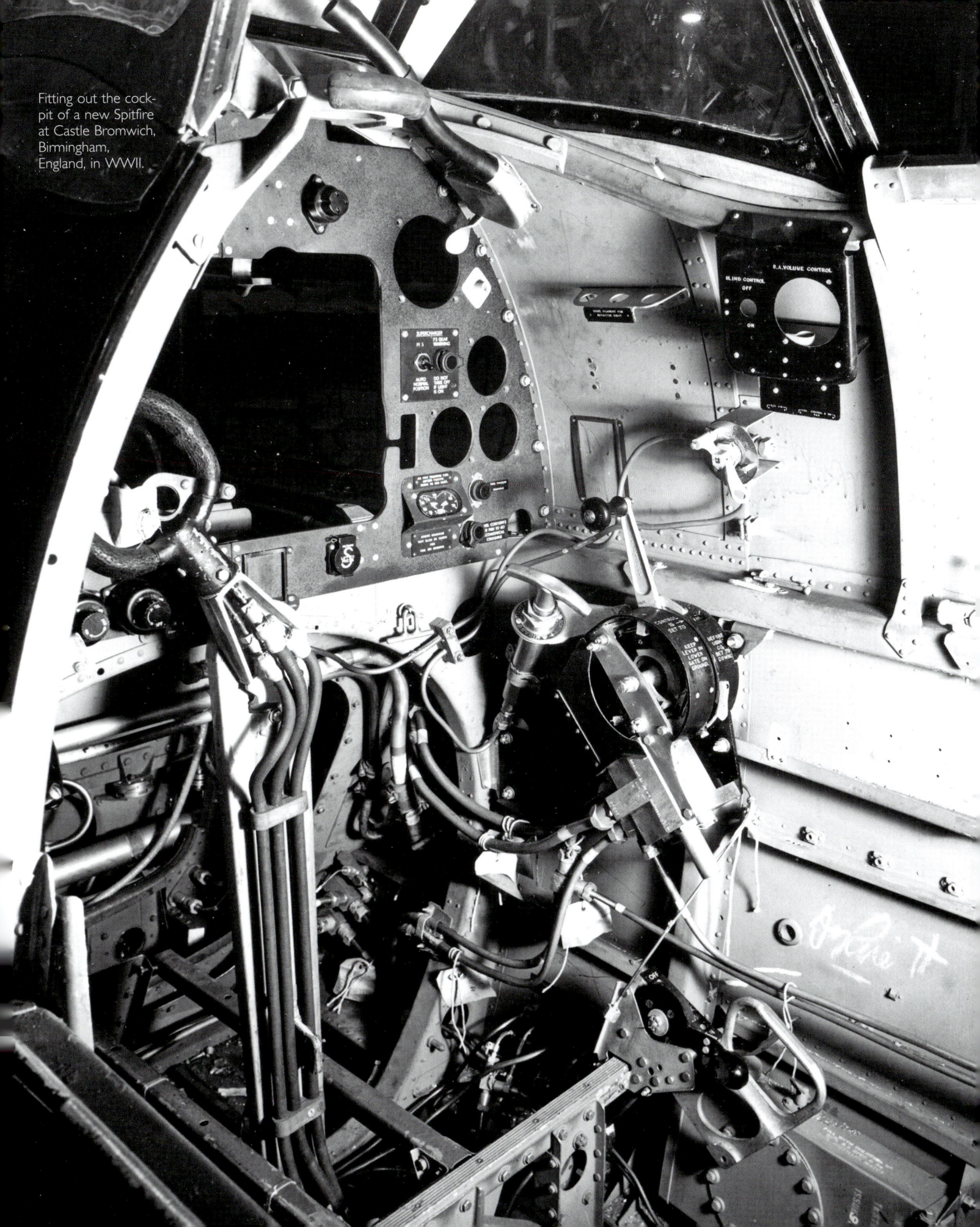

Fitting out the cock-
pit of a new Spitfire
at Castle Bromwich,
Birmingham,
England, in WWII.

MH434, a Mark IX Spitfire of the Old Flying Machine Company, Duxford Airfield, England, had a wartime record of at least eight enemy aircraft downed in combat.

leading role in that effort and caused one Luftwaffe fighter pilot who was defending the Reich in 1945 to comment: "In 1940 Galland was asking for a squadron of Spitfires. Right now I'd sell my soul to the devil for just one Mustang."

For most who flew R. J. Mitchell's wonderful Spitfire, it is their first flight in the type that remains their most enduring memory. John Nesbitt-Dufort: "I strongly suspect that most pilots experienced the same slight feeling of awe as I did when gazing out for the first time over the apparent yards of engine that separated me from the propeller. Brakes on, petrol on, rad shutters open, fine pitch, switches off. I gave her three full dopes on the priming pump, nodded to the airman on the trolley ack and he held his thumb up. 'All clear!' Opening the throttle a shade I threw the booster-coil switch and then ignition, and pressed the starter button. After about two revolutions there was a puff of black smoke as she caught with a roar. I immediately throttled back and switched off the booster-coil. The trolley ack was disconnected and after a brief warming-up, I ran up, checked mags and pitch and then waved away both the chocks and the windswept character who had draped himself over the tail. I saved time by carrying out my preflight checks as I taxied, weaving wildly, to the downwind side of the airfield.

"Coarse weaving was an absolute necessity as the Spit was completely blind dead ahead with the tail down. Stopping the regulation forty-five degrees out of wind I had a final check around the cockpit. Taking a deep breath I gently pushed the handled throttle fully open. There was an immediate and pronounced tendency to swing to the left but this was easily checked by coarse use of opposite rudder, and with a central-ized control column the tail appeared to come up on its own.

"Now for the ticklish part: chang-ing hands. I selected 'up' and with my now free right hand, pumped up the undercarriage avoiding, I hoped successfully, the novice's tendency to pump the control column at the same time. After closing the canopy I adjust-ed boost and revs climbing at 160 mph. This was the fastest aeroplane that I had ever flown and I was duly impressed; throttling back to cruising boost and revs I felt all the controls in turn, elevators very light, ailerons and rudder not quite so light but all sensi-tive and very positive. All the controls stiffened up appreciably, but in no way unpleasantly, as the speed built

The Lockheed P-38 Lightning twin-engined fighter per-formed relatively well in the ETO, but did much better in the Pacific air war against the Japanese.

up. Medium and steep turns in either direction and then daringly a roll—she went round as though she had been on rails! The little aeroplane handled beautifully, her flying characteristics what one might expect from such delightful lines.

"Time to come in again. I located myself quite a distance from the airfield and closed the throttle to test for a stall with the gear and flaps up. Even with the nose held fairly high the speed took a long time to fall off, then after a definite shudder the nose dropped smartly but cleanly at just under eighty-four mph. 'Ye Gods,' I thought, 'that's a bit quick.' For some silly unknown reason, I didn't test for a stall with gear and flaps down, which would have reassured me, but instead headed to

join in the circuit with about twenty pupils in Oxfords and Harvards making frantic darts at the ground with varying degrees of success.

"In those days air traffic was not controlled from the tower—it was just a case of everyone for himself and devil take the hindmost. I reduced speed, pumped down the under-carriage, and slid back the cockpit canopy. Then, by dint of a rather split-arse final turn in at about 130 mph, I insinuated myself in between two indignant Harvards and after snapping down the flaps, came whistling in at 100 mph over the hedge. Far too fast! I floated, pump-handling furiously across two-thirds of the field to eventually sit down firmly at just over 72 mph to finish my run only twenty

yards from the boundary. I was sweating profusely and more than somewhat ashamed of my performance; still, with not a little pride I made the first entry of the magic words 'Spitfire Mk 1, No N3174' in my logbook."

Flying the Spitfire in combat was a different matter entirely, and those who flew both Hurricanes and Spitfires into battle often swear allegiance to one type or the other, an argument further complicated by later developments of both types. While the Hurricane advanced from eight machine guns to twelve, and from twelve machine guns to four cannon, its basic airframe remained largely unchanged. The Spitfire, however, was developed far beyond the original Mitchelll concept at

Supermarine and Vickers-Supermarine. Extended wingtips, clipped wingtips, high-back fuselages, bubble canopies, advanced Merlin and Griffon engines . . . all were implemented as wartime advances of this versatile RAF fighter.

New Zealander Al Deere flew many Spitfire marks into combat through the course of the war. He has no doubt about its superiority over the Messerschmitt ME 109. "The Spitfire was a better aircraft than the 109; not in all respects but overall a better aircraft. Anything the 109 could do, we could do better . . . except a dive. They could run away from us then, but in a turn or a sustained climb we could match them. Top speed or cruise was much the same, but the Spitfire just had the edge."

In the argument over the relative merits of Spitfire versus Hurricane, only the relative viewpoints of the pilots who flew them are normally considered. Former fitter with No 145 (Hurricane) Squadron, Eric Marsden: "If we'd had nothing but Spits, we'd have lost the fight in 1940. The turn-around time on the ground was so poor that Jerry couldn't have failed to get us. The Spit I and II took twenty-six minutes to turn around, compared to a Hurri's nine minutes . . . that is, complete service—re-arm, refuel, and replenish oxygen—from down to up again."

Formerly with the RAF Battle of Britain Memorial Flight, Squadron Leader Paul Day makes a rapid professional evaluation of a Spitfire from its cockpit: "The undercarriage lever, where that is positioned is really undesirable. On the pilot's right, it means a change of hand from the control column to operate. Not a good idea." Slapping the curved pieces of the canopy front, he points out that they too are a cause for concern: "The glass is contoured and not of

An assembly line of North American Aviation P-51 Mustangs in a WWII California plant.

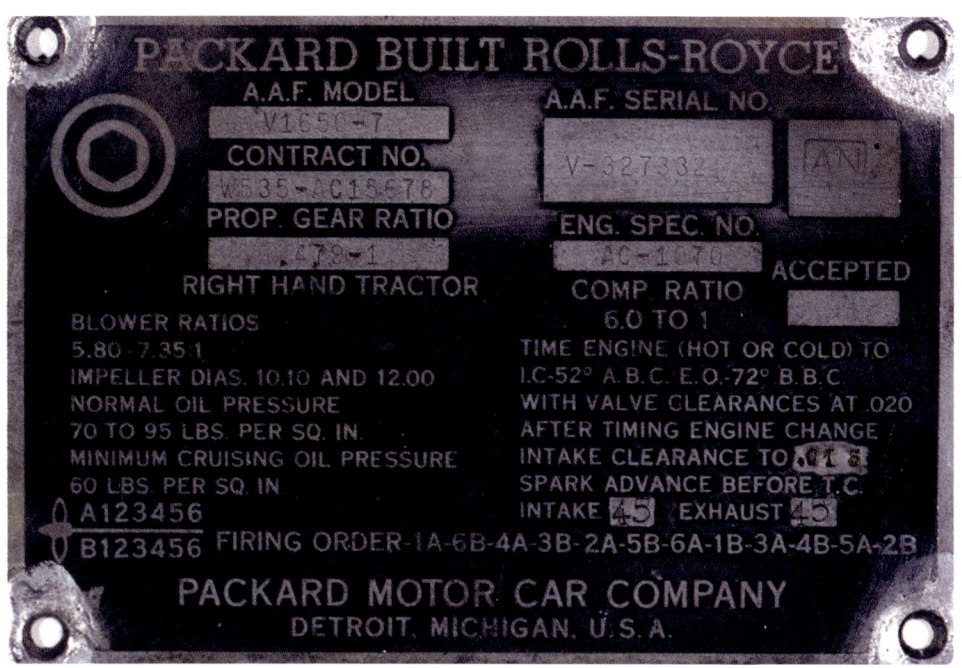

PACKARD BUILT ROLLS-ROYCE

A.A.F. MODEL
V1650-7

A.A.F. SERIAL NO.
V-327332

CONTRACT NO.
W535-AC15678

PROP. GEAR RATIO
.479-1

ENG. SPEC. NO.
AC-1070

RIGHT HAND TRACTOR

ACCEPTED

COMP. RATIO
6.0 TO 1

BLOWER RATIOS
5.80-7.35:1
IMPELLER DIAS. 10.10 AND 12.00
NORMAL OIL PRESSURE
70 TO 95 LBS. PER SQ. IN.
MINIMUM CRUISING OIL PRESSURE
60 LBS. PER SQ. IN.

TIME ENGINE (HOT OR COLD) TO
I.C-52° A.B.C. E.O.-72° B.B.C.
WITH VALVE CLEARANCES AT .020
AFTER TIMING ENGINE CHANGE
INTAKE CLEARANCE TO .018
SPARK ADVANCE BEFORE T.C.
INTAKE 45 EXHAUST 45

A123456
B123456   FIRING ORDER-1A-6B-4A-3B-2A-5B-6A-1B-3A-4B-5A-2B

PACKARD MOTOR CAR COMPANY
DETROIT, MICHIGAN, U.S.A.

left: A Packard manufacturer's identity plate from a license-built Rolls-Royce Merlin engine of a P-51 Mustang escort fighter; below: A Hawker Typhoon fighter as photographed by Charles E. Brown; far right: A weather-beaten leather flying glove found by the author on a hardstand at a former Eighth Air Force airfield in the English Midlands.

good optical quality. That plays all sorts of tricks from a cockpit where visibility should be of paramount importance, but turns out to be a real problem. For instance, up front that whacking great engine obscures most of the sky. At five hundred feet, for example, you are blind for three miles ahead of you. Then, what is going on beneath those wings? Miles of airspace obscured by them. Looking behind, well, that's a real labor of love. There is a teeny makeup mirror for rearward vision but that's of little practical value. As for the instrument panel, not badly laid out, but all the engine instruments are grouped to the right. They aren't terribly eye-catching. In a tight spot, all sorts of things could be going on there which you might not notice. The system for arming and firing, though, is simple, effective, and good.''

Summing up, and despite his dislikes, Day felt that "Mitchell had got it right." Given the technology of the late 1930s, it is surely a fair view. . . especially when set against Day's evaluation of the Messerschmitt ME 109. It was, after all, how the Spitfire shaped up against the 109 that counted. Lowering himself into the 109 cockpit, Day's opinion of the little fighter was quickly formed. As he closed the heavily-framed hood, he described it as ''like a modified Kaiser's helmet.''

''Well, good grief! It's terrible. Not for the squeamishly claustrophobic. There is twenty-five percent less working room in here and up front the vision is even worse. All you can see is Krupp of Essen. Looking behind is a hundred percent worse than in a Spit.'' Squadron Leader Day had never flown the Messerschmitt, but in delivering his verdict he was absolutely certain: ''I wouldn't choose to go to war in one given that the opposition had Spitfires.''

Geoffrey Page flew the Hawker Hurricane in combat with No 56 Squadron, RAF: ''In the Hurricane we knew that the ME 109 could outdive us, but not out-turn us. With that knowledge one obviously used the turning maneuver rather than trying to beat the man at the game in which he was clearly superior. With a 109 sitting behind you, you'd stay in a really tight turn and after a few turns the positions would be reversed and you'd be on his tail. In short, I'd say that the Hurricane was a magnificent aeroplane to go to war in.''

The twin-engined, fork-tailed Lockheed P-38 Lightning was, perhaps, the most revolutionary Allied fighter of the war. But while the airplane was novel in concept and appearance, the Lightning's performance in the European air war was less than brilliant. Brought to Britain for the long-range bomber escort work in the summer of 1943, it had the range advantage over the Republic P-47 Thunderbolt; it could take the ''Big Friends'' deeper into enemy territory. Many pilots who

flew the Lightning on operations from England had mixed feelings about it. Royal Frey, former curator of the U.S. Air Force Museum, Wright-Patterson Air Force Base, Ohio, flew the P-38 with the 20th Fighter Group from Kings Cliffe and Wittering in World War II: ''With its tricycle gear, counter-rotating props, muffled engine exhaust through the turbos, and fairly heavy weight, the P-38 was a sheer delight on takeoff. You would take the runway, line up, brake to a full stop and advance the throttles to at least forty-four inches of manifold pressure, to where the turbos would cut in. The nose would gradually drop as the increasing pull of the props forced the nose strut to compress, and the whole plane would shake and vibrate. A quick glance at the instrument panel and off the brakes. Up popped the nose and you bounded forward like a racehorse from the starting gate.

''As you gathered speed down the runway, the heavy weight of the plane deadened any bumps and you felt as if you were in a Cadillac. The turbo

Major Hayley Aycock, CO of the 324th Bomb Squadron, 91st Bomb Group, has a final pre-mission word with 1st Lt. J. M. Smith, the pilot of the B-17 *Our Gang*, before the bomber departs from their Bassingbourn, England base.

exhausts made the engines sound extremely muffled, as in a high-powered pleasure boat—no loud cracking or roar so usual in those days of reciprocating engines. No torque to swing the nose and beautiful visibility down the runway from the level attitude of the tricycle gear. At seventy mph you gently eased back on the control yoke, and at ninety-five to a hundred mph the plane lifted softly into the air. What complete comfort for a combat plane.

"With its inherent stability the P-38 was extremely easy to fly and once trimmed for straight and level flight, it was a hands-off airplane. If you put it into an unusual attitude (within reasonable limits) and then got off the controls, it would slowly waddle and oscillate around in the air and eventually return to straight and level flight. This was because its center of lift was above its center of gravity, i.e. most of the mass of the airplane was slung under a wing having a large amount of dihedral. Other fighters of the era tended to drop off on one wing or the other.

"The Lightning was an excellent gun platform, although it was more difficult than in a P-47 or P-51 to get strikes on a target because the four .50 caliber guns and one 20mm cannon were grouped so closely together in the nose. However, if we got any strikes at all, we had a much better chance of getting a victory—those five weapons put out such a heavy column of projectiles that they bored a large hole through anything they hit.

"The P-38 also had the famous Fowler flap, which at half-extended position, greatly decreased turn radius at altitude, with very little additional drag. Incorporated into the P-38 for combat this feature was given the name 'maneuver flaps,' and with it I actually turned with late-mod-

el Spitfires during 'rat races' over England, and turned inside Fw 190s in action over Europe.

"Although the Lightning could turn very tightly once it got into a bank, getting it into the bank was another matter. Late K and L series Lightnings had aileron boost, but this feature came too late for those of us who took on the Luftwaffe deep inside Germany in late 1943 and 1944. Because of the weight of the plane and the poor leverage of a control wheel compared to that of a control stick, the Lightning's roll rate approximated that of a pregnant whale. If we ever got behind a single-engine fighter in a tight turn, all the other pilot had to do was flip into an opposite turn and dive, by the time we had banked and turned after him, he was practically out of sight.

"In addition to an agonizingly slow roll rate, the P-38s I flew in combat had two other very limiting features—restricted dive and extremely low cockpit temperature. It was suicide to put the P-38 into a near-vertical dive at high altitude; all we P-38 pilots knew it, and I believe all the Luftwaffe pilots knew it, for they usually used the vertical dive to escape from us. You could 'split-S' and do other vertical-type maneuvers at high altitude, as long as you continued to pull the nose through the vertical, you always held your airspeed within limits. But let the nose stay in the vertical position for more than a few seconds and the nose would actually 'tuck under' beyond the vertical position, and it would be impossible to recover from its dive. The only salvation was to pop the canopy, release your seat belt, and hope you would clear the plane as you were sucked from the cockpit. The 20th Group lost two P-38s in vertical dives over England before we went operational, but both pilots bailed out successfully.

"The other limiting feature, cockpit temperature, would be more correctly identified as paralyzing. Cockpit heat from the engine manifolds was non-existent. When you were at thirty thousand feet on bomber escort and the air temperature was -55°F outside the cockpit, it was -55°F inside the cockpit. After thirty minutes or so at such a temperature, a pilot became so numb that he was too miserable to be of any real value; to make matters worse, he did not particularly care. Only his head and neck, exposed to the direct rays of the sun, retained any warmth.

"Not only did the numbness seriously decrease a pilot's efficiency, the bulky clothing he wore further restricted his efforts. For example, I wore double-thickness silk gloves, then heavy chamois gloves, and topped these with heavy leather gauntlets (all British issue). Inside all these layers were fingers almost frozen stiff and completely without feeling. Flipping a single electrical switch required deep concentration, skill, and luck, and the P-38 cockpit was loaded with electrical switches. How we envied the P-47 and P-51 pilots with a heat-producing engine in front of them to maintain a decent cockpit temperature.

"Admittedly, the P-38 was outperformed by the P-47 and P-51 in the skies over Europe, but many of its difficulties were the result of unnecessary design deficiencies and the slow pace of both the AAF and Lockheed in correcting them. One can only ponder about how much more rapidly the troubles would have been remedied if the slide-rule types had been flying the plane in combat against the Luftwaffe. But I will always remember the P-38 with the greatest fondness. Even with all her idiosyncrasies, she was a real dream to fly."

The crumbling, derelict Flying Control tower at the former RAF Tangmere fighter station in southern England.

GROUND GRIPPER

STAFF SERGEANT MERLE OLMSTED was an aircraft mechanic serving with the 362nd Fighter Squadron of the 357th Fighter Group, Eighth U.S. Army Air Force, at Leiston, England, in World War II. He rose to assistant crew chief and later to crew chief, responsible for a P-51D Mustang escort fighter. "Aircraft Maintenance—in those days it was called the Engineering Section—consisted of the flight-line crews, usually three men: two mechanics (the crew chief and assistant crew chief) and an armorer. For every four aircraft there was a flight chief to coordinate requirements and activities. Then there were two hangar crews, each operating on twelve-hour shifts. They did things that could not be done out on the line, such as engine changes. Assigned to the hangar crews were an electrician and a propeller man. Each squadron also had its assigned painter and carpenter. For heavy maintenance, we had the 469th Service Squadron on base. They were not part of the fighter group, but were certainly part of the 'family.'

"We were always busy, routinely so. There was some boredom broken by occasional excitement. The schedule of the flight-line crews depended on the briefing times for the pilots. The mechanics were awakened each morning by the CQ, who turned on the lights and always said something like : 'Briefing at 0730, maximum effort, maximum range.' We usually, but not always, went to breakfast first. Often, one of the two of us would go directly to the aircraft and start the preflight while the other one went to breakfast first. That way one of us would be at the airplane all the time. On arriving there, all aircraft covers

A cannon-armed Spitfire ready to leave on a ground-attack run into Germany.

The control tower at the former Goxhill fighter station near Hull, England; below right: Tower personnel at an American fighter base in wartime England.

would be removed and a walk-around inspection made to see if any leaks had developed overnight. Drop tanks, which had been fitted the night before, were fueled. The propeller was pulled through four to six blades. The battery cart was hooked up and the engine was started for a brief run-up to high power, to check mag drop, pressure, and temperatures. The fuel selector was switched to the left and right tanks to draw fuel into the lines, which would make the engine cut out a few times until the lines were full . . . which was why this little operation had to be done on the ground. With these essential preparations complete, there remained other work to be done before the pilots came to their planes.

"The tanks would be topped off to replace the few gallons used in the run-up. About then the armorer would arrive to charge the guns. When his preflight was completed, there was just enough time for last-minute details like polishing the windshield and canopy. Smears or specks on the Plexiglas caused distractions and distortions, and sometimes recriminations from the pilots. Worse, such seemingly minor flaws might lead to a pilot not coming home. The ground crews did their best to maintain the aircraft perfectly for their pilots.

"The pilot would arrive and I would help strap him in and hook up. Then it was start-up time, the chocks were pulled from the wheels, the Mustang taxied out to its assigned position for takeoff. Then, they were gone. My buddies and I would watch them go with a sense of relief and not a little envy.

"Now it was time to sit around and sweat it out. Free time for the ground crews. Since the planes were usually gone during the noon hour, we would go to midday chow. I remember that the food was not really bad, considering the circumstances, but being a picky eater I passed up the meals I didn't like. If the mission being flown was an especially rough one the waiting ground

WIRELESS (M&C) TOOL BOX USED BY CPL W RAY 1940–1945 ALL ITEMS ARE GENUINE AND MARKED A M (DSR)

A specialized tool kit for use on an RAF Hurricane fighter; right: The Ops Room state board at the former Little Walden Mustang base near Saffron Walden, Essex, England.

crews might not be too hungry. When I didn't care for the chow, I would go over to the small PX on the base and make do with a candy bar. An officer presided over that PX and, as he appeared to have very little to do, I decided that the next time around I would like to be a PX officer. Then it was time to get back to the flight line so I walked, biked, or caught a ride out for the final wait.

"The way the aircraft looked as they returned told the ground crews a lot. Were they in the same formation as at departure, or were they straggling in? Where was Joan and what was wrong with Rolla V? Was that Floogie II doing a victory roll? Soon they were all back—at least all those who were coming back.

"As the Mustangs rolled into the dispersals the gun muzzles were observed to see if the red tape covers had been shot away, indicating combat. A final blip of throttle brought each fighter swinging around to a stop on the hardstand. The propeller would mill to a stop, the canopy back and harness undone, greetings were shouted between pilot and ground crewmen. 'Did you get anything?' 'What happened to Joan?' 'Any defects, sir?' As the pilot climbed from his cockpit and went off to debriefing, the ground crew was already at work . . . covers off the guns . . . postflight checks . . . new drop tanks fitted . . . oil washed from the crankcase breather. Popping and cracking as the hot engine cooled, our plane sat on its concrete pan and we

replaced the covers on the canopy and pitot tube, secured the control locks in place, and, finally, went off to evening chow. Then back to our living quarters. Maybe there would be a chance to get away from the base for a few hours. Tomorrow would be just the same as today. The food, the cold, the mud, and, really, a lot of satisfaction in the jobs we were doing. That experience was one of the high points of my life."

Eighteen-year-old Eric Marsden was posted to 145 Squadron at Kenley as a fitter IIE just before the Battle of Britain. "When I got there I found out they had gone! Someone thought that 145 had gone to Croydon, but when I got there the afterguard was all that was left. No 145 had moved

on to Filton, but we were to go down to Tangmere the next day where the squadron was to be based."

In view of the frantic and confused military situation of the period, the bureaucracy that had left Eric chasing 145 around southern England may be excused. The squadron was soon to be whipped into an efficient unit. Ultimately, that efficiency would mean a squadron of serviceable Hurricanes with confident and combat-ready pilots. Certainly the glamour and recognition would go to the pilots, the commanding officer and flight commanders, but serviceability and the pilot's confidence and feeling of security about the aircraft would be seen to by the ground crews. Just as the pilots were molded into a battle "team" by the squadron and flight commanders, the ground crews were led and inspired by effective leaders. The officer-in-charge was the engineering officer, but each of the squadron's flights, A and B, had its NCO-in-charge. Eric was in B Flight.

"The NCO-in-charge was known as Chiefy, even to his face, once one was accepted. Irreverently, this particular one was known as Jesus from his cherubic face and halo of golden curls, albeit thinning from advanced age. He was in his thirties.

"On the early Hurricanes the compressed-air system was maintained in flight by a BTH compressor. We had to check the oil level through a spring-loaded plunger and the only way of getting the castor oil in was with the flight's one and only syringe. It could take quite a time to go to the store, find that the syringe was out, and then track it down along the flight line. Then there were the cowlings. The top engine cowlings, and the extra-thick cowl over the fuselage tank, could be absolute pigs

Ground personnel awaiting the return of their group aircraft from a mission; right: The Ops Room state board at Eighth Air Force Headquarters near High Wycombe, Bucks.

to replace. Fitting them was an art involving heavy blows with the flat of the hand in just the right places, and most were individual to particular kites. Sometimes cowling up after a daily inspection could take longer than the inspection itself. Daily inspections were the routine checks that each aeroplane was subjected to to keep it in top order, with each prescribed check meticulously entered in the aircraft's logbook. RAF Form 700 had to be signed and countersigned. I was 'engines' but I had a rigger as a partner for the Dis. We each had our own specified jobs according to our trade schedules. Check all fastenings, pipe joints, etc. Check and top up oil, fuel, coolant, oxygen. Such routine, however, was not without its problems. Every Hurricane built was equipped with a special Hawker tool, a combined tank-cap key / screwdriver to fit the fasteners of the removable cowlings, panels, and fairings. Unfortunately, everyone down the delivery chain, from manufacturer to squadron, was convinced they had to have one. That meant that we who really needed to have one didn't. We had to make do. But lack of proper equipment to do the job was not confined to just specialized tools. We couldn't get soft cloth or Perspex polish for the Perspex and glass of the cockpits and had to use our own Bluebell or Brasso and whatever rags we could scrounge up. One day, our flight commander came back in a towering rage. Instead of getting down from his kite he ordered the rigger and myself up onto the wing. 'Look at that,' he said, pointing to the tiniest speck in the righthand lower corner of the windscreen. 'I've had the entire flight chasing that damned speck all over France.' He tore us off a proper strip, but when Chiefy explained the

shortages he vanished in the direction of the Stores. Presumably he expressed his opinions in a similar fashion because after that there were no more shortages of these materials.

"Actually, the ground crews practically worshipped their pilots. By July and August of 1940 our pilots were getting distinctly 'frayed around the edges' and I knew that one or two considered themselves 'write-offs.' It didn't affect their flying or their attitude to fighting—it was just that they no longer had any hope of survival for themselves. It was grievous for us on the ground. We could do little to help. We couldn't take their places—though most of us would have given anything for the chance—and it probably wouldn't be incorrect to say that our respect and liking for our pilots almost became a kind of love at this time. We had to watch them—indeed, help them—take off to go and die in ones and twos. To make matters worse, the fitters, riggers, armorers, and aircraft hands of 145 could often hear their pilots in action, fighting and dying. A loudspeaker above the crewroom door allowed us to hear the radio chatter between our pilots in the air, sometimes a facility of dubious value. Hearing someone you like in dire trouble can be quite unfunny."

For the ground types like Eric, there was no socializing with the pilots. The pilots were mostly officers. The ground crews who toiled under the hot sun, in freezing cold and rain, with bloodied fingers and soiled clothes, were a breed apart. They were "other ranks" or NCOs, and RAF protocol and King's Regulations forbade fraternization between them and the officers. Nevertheless, a friendliness that stopped just short of familiarity transcended the taboos of officialdom. "We ground crew had a good relationship with our pilots. Not of the 'Hi Mac' variety,

An American armorer loads linked .50 caliber machine-gun ammunition on the wing of a P-51B Mustang fighter.

Field maintenance on a P-38 Lightning fighter in wartime England.

as with our U.S. friends later in the war . . . but they did take the trouble to know us by name and we could—and did—talk with them about the war, the squadron affairs and the daily round." Thumbing his nose at authority, and crossing the officer-other ranks divide, Pilot Officer Roy Marchand, a Hurricane pilot with 73 Squadron, recalled his feeling for his own "nuts-and-bolts" team in a letter home that he concluded with: "Must close now. I want to go and stand my fitter and rigger a beer or two. Boy, they deserve it."

The privilege of rank and flying was not all that separated the pilots from the "erks." There was also the pay. If the pilot's pay was poor, then that given to the lesser mortals on the ground must be classed as miserly. Eric Marsden: "As Leading Aircraftsman / Flight Mechanic, I think I was then on three shillings and sixpence per day. That's what it was in 1939 as an RAF (Volunteer Reserve) Fitter IIE Under Training. Some time after the war started we were told that we had been remustered as Flight Mechanics (Under Training) at two shillings per day and we would have to repay the difference from September 2nd in deductions! This meant that for some time we got only one shilling and sixpence per day—the service minimum upon which it was reckoned that we could clean our shoes and buttons. It made you glad to be a volunteer and not a conscript . . ." At that time, the most junior rank of pilot officer in the General Duties (Flying) branch of the RAF (VR) could expect to pocket the princely sum of eleven shillings per day.

At the height of that summer 145 Squadron was operating from Westhampnett, a small grass airfield just down the road from Tangmere (which controlled Westhampnett

administratively). It was here that Eric grew to know his pilots. "There was Flight Lieutenant Adrian Boyd, the B Flight commander, 'Boydy' to one and all. For me he has always been one of the great pilots of the war—as much for his ability to lead and train men, as for his ability as a fighter pilot. If his scores were not up with the top aces, this was undoubtedly through his habit of crediting 'kills' to beginner pilots. Another was Pilot Officer Nigel Weir. He was very keen to get a German Mae West life jacket. They were considered far superior to the RAF-issue ones and highly prized. Nigel was so anxious to get his that he landed in a field alongside a German kite he had shot down. He must have startled the farmer's wife by borrowing a bucket in which to carry the prize home between his legs on the floor of the Hurricane. It was somewhat bloody and he had it soaking in water, but he wore it with considerable pride once it was cleaned up. Another favorite among the ground crews of 145 was a Pole, Flight Lieutenant Pankratz. Whenever he was asked how many Jerries he had shot down in a fight, he would say: "I'm not interested in how many I have shot down—only in how many are left.'"

Ten Little Fighter boys taking off in Line / One was in coarse pitch, then there were nine / Nine little fighter boys climbing "through the gate," / One's petrol wasn't on, then there were eight / Eight little fighter boys scrambling up to heaven / One weaver didn't and then there were seven / Seven little fighter boys up to all the tricks / One had a hangover then there were six / Six little fighter boys milling over Hythe / One's pressure wasn't up and then there were five / Five little fighter boys over France's shore / One flew reciprocal and then there were four / Four little fighter boys joining in the spree / One's sight wasn't on and then there were three / Three little fighter boys high up in the blue / One's rubber pipe was loose and then there were two / Two little fighter boys homing out of sun / Flew straight and level and then there was one / One little fighter boy happy to be home / Beat up the dispersal and then there were none.

"We always had the very comforting feeling that our Spitfires were maintained as perfectly as was humanly possible. I don't think my engine ever missed a beat throughout the whole summer, and this means a terrific lot to you when you are continually going into action and any mechanical failure will have the most unpleasant consequences."
—Flight Lieutenant D. M. Crook

"Sometimes you waited and they didn't come back. Sometimes your plane came back and you saw others waiting and theirs didn't come back. Fortunately, although the planes didn't back, quite often the pilots did. In fact, one time . . . it was at Elm Park underground station, and two of our pilots came up out of the station with their parachutes tucked under their arms. They'd come back from their sorties by underground."
—Dave Davies, AC1 Engine Fitter, 232 (Natal) Squadron

left: Field engine work on a P-47 Thunderbolt; below: Replacing the flak-damaged vertical stabilizer of a B-17 bomber with that of a "hangar queen" at the Ridgewell base of the 381st Bomb Group, Eighth U.S. Army Air Force.

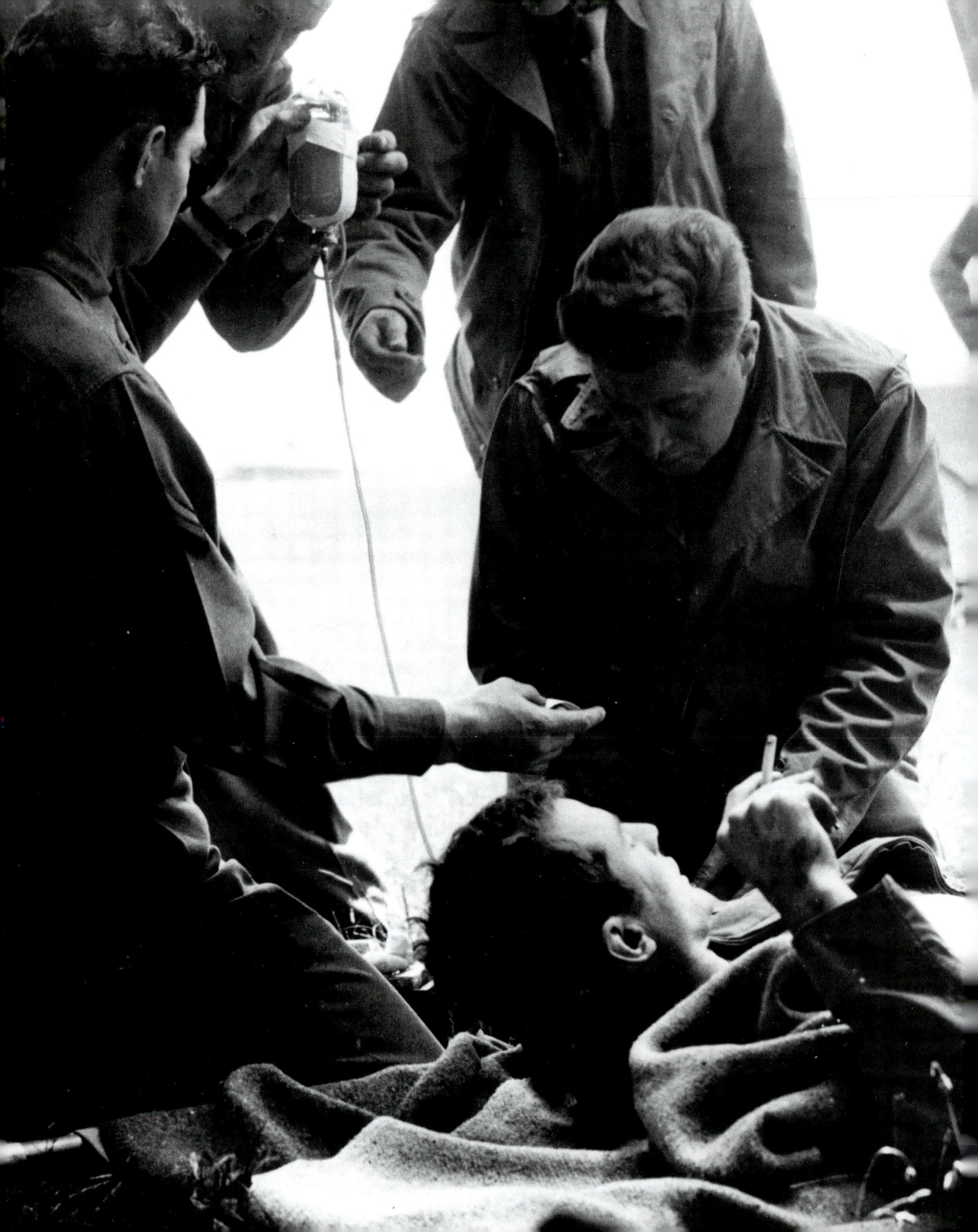

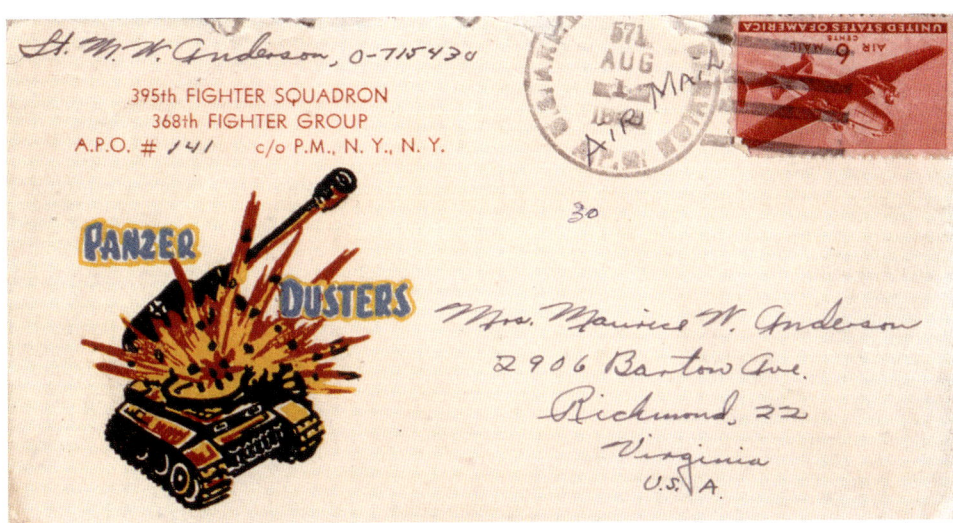

A flight surgeon meets this returning bomber and attends to a wounded gunner under the wing of the aircraft before taking him to the base hospital for additional treatment.

They shall renew their strength and mount up on wings like eagles.

This generation of Americans has a rendezvous with destiny.
—Franklin D. Roosevelt

Wake, friend, from forth thy lethargy! The drum beats brave and loud in Europe, and bids come all that dare rouse: or are not loathe to quit their viscious ease, and be o'erwhelmed with it. It is a call to keep the spirits alive that gasp for action, and would yet revive man's buried honour, in his sleepy life.
—from *An Epistle to a Friend, to Persuade Him to the Wars* by Ben Jonson

AMERICAN FIGHTER PILOTS had been serving with the Royal Air Force since the first year of the war. Their numbers remain a disputed issue since in order to circumvent the U.S. Neutrality Act many assumed Canadian or South African nationality.

Charles Sweeny, a wealthy American businessman living in London in 1940, had noted the growing number of American volunteer fliers coming to England and began organizing them into a cohesive fighting unit—the Eagle Squadron. Approved by the British Air Ministry in September 1940, the Eagles were to operate within their own exclusive squadrons in RAF Fighter Command, numbers 71, 121, and 133. The first of the Eagles, 71 Squadron, was formed with Hurricanes at Kirton-in-Lindsey, Lincolnshire.

In the United States a clandestine organization known as the Clayton Knight Committee helped and advised prospective candidates to become Eagles. Then, from Canada, the fledglings had to run the transatlantic gauntlet of U-boats before actual-

ly becoming Eagles in Britain. And there were other obstacles. James A. Gray joined No 71 Squadron via the Clayton Knight organization. "It was a curious situation. I didn't have to register for the draft . . . so I didn't have a draft notice . . . so I wasn't trying to avoid the draft, which a number of chaps were. I had been flying out of Oakland Airport where I soloed, and then went to the University of California where I joined the Civil Pilot Training Program and got myself another hundred hours or so of flying time. About then, word was circulated around Oakland Airport that the British were recruiting for the RAF. It was sort of subrosa, though, because they really weren't allowed to. I had applied to the Army Air Corps and been turned down, and I was really eager to fly with an air force—any air force. So, I signed up. I took some exams from a retired Air Corps major who was a medico down in Berkeley. Then I was assigned to Bakersfield on July 1, 1940."

Four schools were set up for training pilots in the United States, as a part of the British Refresher Training Course: at Dallas, Texas; Tulsa, Oklahoma; Glendale and Bakersfield, California. They provided 80 percent of the ultimate total of 243 Eagle Squadron pilots. Jim Gray recalled his fourteen-day voyage from Halifax, Nova Scotia, to England: "It was a boat which used to ply the Caribbean. About five days out of Liverpool a huge storm developed and our old banana boat just couldn't keep formation with the convoy of some eighty or so ships. The deal was that everyone would keep formation on the slowest ship in the convoy. About eight knots. Well, the commodore of the convoy radioed that everyone was on their own, and, for about four days, we were just that. On our own.

Captain Don Gentile and his P-51 Mustang *Shangri-La* at Debden.

EARLY AMERICAN

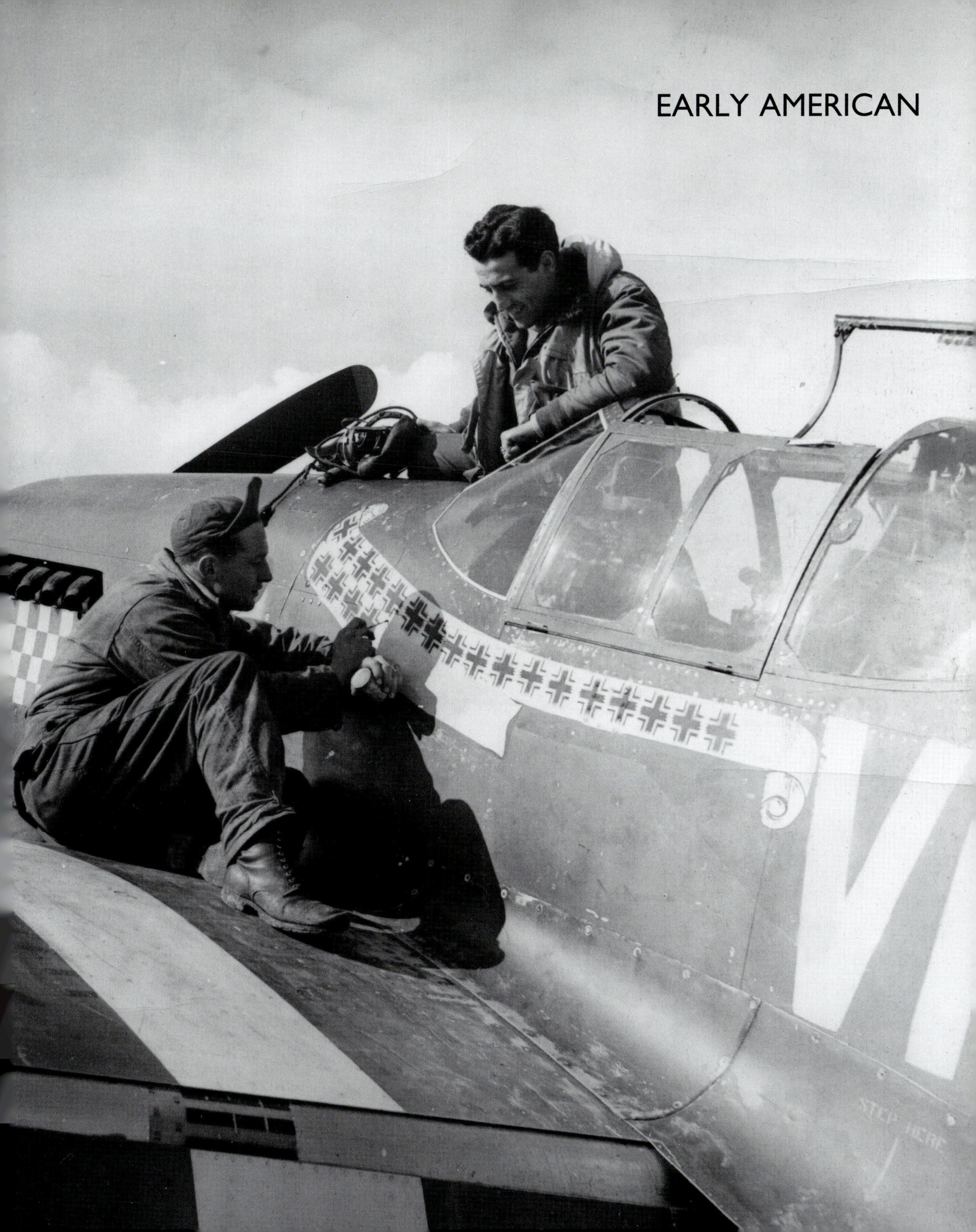

The perimeter track at the Raydon, Suffolk base of the 353rd, 357th, and 358th Fighter Groups in the Second World War; right: A wartime T2 hangar on the Raydon base.

We were a little nervous because some time earlier, a ship in another convoy had been torpedoed and had gone down with some prospective Eagle types on it. Eleven were rescued but five were lost."

Safely in London and still officially civilians, the new Eagles were quickly fitted for RAF uniforms at Moss Bros clothing store and given the most junior rank of Pilot Officer. From Number 3 Personnel Reception Centre at Bournemouth they were sent to Number 56 Operational Training Unit (OTU) at Sutton Bridge, Norfolk. Graduating as a fighter pilot, Jim Gray was posted to 71 Squadron,

Martlesham Heath, Suffolk, its new base, in December 1941. The relatively new squadron had seen action since February 5, 1941.

Other American pilots had already been flying and fighting with the Royal Air Force, Red Tobin, Shorty Keough, Andy Mamedoff, Billy Fiske, and Hack Russell among them. Fiske died in the Battle of Britain, and Russell had been killed over the beaches of Dunkirk. Mamedoff, Keough, and Tobin were all killed later in the war.

Problems plagued the Eagle Squadrons from the beginning. The RAF was extremely wary of American leadership of any of its squadrons.

A British officer, Squadron Leader Walter M. Churchill, was put in charge of 71 Squadron. The unit was part of No 12 Group, RAF, which was under the command of Air Vice Marshal Trafford Leigh-Mallory, who had made no secret of his distaste for American fliers in the Royal Air Force. Even the Air Officer Commanding, RAF Fighter Command, Sholto Douglas, expressed reservations about the Eagles to the visiting Commanding General, U.S. Army Air Corps, Henry H. Arnold. The future seemed precarious for the Eagles; and in America, the FBI had been making it difficult for the Clayton Knight Committee to operate, and

had made it known that the Neutrality Act would be strictly enforced. Then, however, Winston Churchill himself intervened in support of Charles Sweeny's original Eagle Squadron concept, which the British Air Council was now opposing. And, in a fortunate decision for the Eagles, 71 Squadron was transferred out of Leigh-Mallory's 12 Group and posted to Martlesham Heath as a part of 11 Group. At last the Eagles were down in the main battle zone and seeing action.

The fortunes of 71 Squadron improved and, with the increasing numbers of American volunteer fighter pilots en route to England, two additional Eagle Squadrons were soon formed—121 at Kirton-in-Lindsey and 133 at Coltishall. Many of the Eagles, and not exclusively those in 71, were to become leading aces in the U.S. Eighth Air Force; Don Blakeslee, Don Gentile, Richard Peterson, and Howard Hively among them.

Jim Gray: "Bob Sprague and I were out on an air-sea rescue duty after a big raid on Düsseldorf. A lot of the bombers were strewn out across the North Sea, so we went to try to locate them and escort Walrus amphibians or ships that might pick the crews up. While we were on this duty, we encountered some ME 109s.

General Dwight Eisenhower presenting awards to Colonel Don Blakeslee and Captain Don Gentile at a Debden ceremony in 1944.

We were at 2,000 feet and a couple of them were flying down below us, so Bob said 'Hey, let's go down and get 'em.' Well, some other 109s joined in the fray and I was kind of circling round when one got on my tail. I shook him off but, as I turned out of it, there was another 109 on Bob's tail, all set to do some damage. Luckily, I was able to position myself well and sent the German splashing into the sea, and the other 109s withdrew. We continued our patrol after that. Bob's number two was a fabulous guy called 'Deacon' Hively who would later achieve fame with the 4th Fighter Group at Debden. This was his first operation."

No 71, the first Eagle Squadron, was getting a lot of attention. But it would not be the first choice of Carroll "Red" McColpin, who considered himself a careful and professional pilot. He wanted to fly and he wanted to fight. But he also wanted to live. In his opinion, there was a certain playboy/adventurer element in 71 Squadron that he didn't trust. He believed that survival in combat depended on the other pilots as well as himself. "I reckoned some of these guys were not proper people. There was a particular gang from Los Angeles in 71 that raised hell, wrote bad checks, got in trouble with the females, and wanted to drink more than they wanted to fly—all that kind of stuff. So, from the OTU I flatly refused a posting to 71 Squadron. Instead, I joined a British squadron."

But after a period of flying Hurricanes with No 607 Squadron in the north of England, McColpin was posted to No 121 (Eagle) Squadron. He saw a lot of action with 121 and earned a reputation as one of the very best of the Eagle pilots. Recognized for his courage and skill in air fighting, he was one of

the first American recipients of the British Distinguished Flying Cross. He was then summoned to see Air Chief Marshal Leigh-Mallory, who had moved from 12 Group to the command of 11 Group. Despite his doubts about the American pilots, Leigh-Mallory now had a job for McColpin to do. He was to be promoted from pilot officer to flight lieutenant, and was to take command of B Flight, 133 Squadron.

McColpin, at twenty-seven, brought a rare maturity to the youthful Eagles. While not doubting that his age and experience contributed to his survival and success, there were other factors that he counted as crucial. "You could still use luck. Every once in a while a part would break or fail on your airplane while you were flying, but you could eliminate or reduce your need for luck by making sure your plane was 100 percent ready to go. Then, as double insurance, you'd always make sure you knew where you were going to land in an emergency."

McColpin's policy was careful planning, and he followed certain personal rules. They included not living it up in the pubs and clubs—all part of maintaining the peak physical condition on which he prided himself. He had first-rate eyesight, good hearing, physical strength . . . and endurance. Four hundred fighter missions without once being hit and never losing a pilot when leading his flight proved the wisdom of his philosophy. His success as flight commander eventually led to his promotion to commander of 133 Squadron. His men admired and respected his leadership qualities. He was once gratified to overhear one of them say, "Well, I'll go with McColpin any place he'll go." "Amen," was the response of the other pilots in the room. But despite this vote of confidence, there was still an occasional

voice of dissent, as when his pilots became aware that pilots in other squadrons were getting quicker promotion. McColpin told them bluntly that he would transfer them if they wanted out, but they should remember one thing: the other outfits were taking the casualties. Did they want to be live pilot officers or dead flight lieutenants?

In the spring of 1942 the Eagle Squadrons were well established, with 71 Squadron at Debden, 121 at North Weald and 133 at Biggin Hill. These were the best, most prestigious stations, in the forefront of Fighter Command's offensive. Under the commands of Gus Daymond, Chesley Peterson, and McColpin, the squadrons had become seasoned and fully effective. They were great favorites of the press, and Hollywood showed interest with a new motion picture, *Eagle Squadron*. Introduced by the popular war correspondent Quentin Reynolds, the cast included Robert Stack, Diana Barrymore, Jon Hall, Eddie Albert, Nigel Bruce, Leif Erikson, John Loder . . . and the Eagles themselves. Most of the action was filmed at the actual bases of the Eagle Squadrons in England, but the filmmakers hadn't appreciated or accounted for the reality of war. Every time a pilot was lost, the script had to be rewritten and previously exposed footage had to be scrapped. In the end the filmmakers gave up and moved the production back to Hollywood. The resulting movie was a schmaltzy, romanticized disaster. It was too much for the assembled Eagles to stomach and most of them walked out of its London premiere, even though the king was present.

After the United States' entry into the war, the transfer of the Eagles into the U.S. Eighth Air Force was eventually agreed on and, by

September 1942, was under way. Some Eagle pilots were wearing U.S. olive drab uniforms alongside others still in RAF blue. Transfer to the Army Air Force meant better pay; however, not all of the Eagles would move over to the Eighth, despite this and the generally improved conditions available in American service. Jim Gray recalled that there was and is a general misconception about the pilots having to transfer over. "They gave us the opportunity to transfer or not. I opted not to. Everybody thought you had to transfer over to the American Air Force at a certain point if you were American. Not at all. There were about six or seven of us that didn't transfer—Art Roscoe, Leo Nomis, and Jimmy Nelson among them."

It wasn't the same for everyone. Red McColpin: "I knew that a big mission to Morlaix was coming up, but I'd been ordered to transfer to the USAAF. Ordered. I kept delaying it week after week. We were down at Biggin Hill, but 133 was being moved up to Great Sampford near Debden. The mission was being laid on . . . then off . . . then on again. I decided I wouldn't go and leave the outfit until the mission was over with. I was gonna lead that mission. Then General 'Monk' Hunter called up from Fighter Command Headquarters of the Eighth Air Force and said, 'I understand you haven't transferred,' and I said, 'Yes sir.' He just said, 'Well, you get your butt in there and transfer, right now!' To which I came back, 'Sir, I'm waiting for this Morlaix mission and I'm trying to keep enough boys in here to run it 'cause it's a big one.' 'To hell with that . . . you get in there and transfer,' Hunter replied. 'Well, sir,' I said, 'you understand that I'm in the Royal Air Force, and I have an ops instruction which says we are going to Morlaix

when they lay it on. I'm the CO here and I've got my squadron on the line.' With that he snorted and hung up. About an hour later I got a call from an air marshal in the group. 'McColpin, do you take orders from me?' I said 'I certainly do, yes sir.' That's how I came to transfer over."

The Morlaix raid, when it came, was a disaster. It was a sad way for the Eagle Squadrons to bow out of the RAF. Gordon Brettell, a British pilot, was placed in command of 133 Squadron, and led the Morlaix mission on September 26, 1942, in Red McColpin's place.

The Morlaix raid required the Eagles to escort American bombers hitting the Brest peninsula, flying out across the widest part of the Channel, over a heavily defended area and back again. By this time 133 Squadron was at Great Sampford in Essex, waiting to be absorbed into the USAAF . . . but would still fly the mission. To that end, the unit was sent to Bolt Head, a forward base located between Dartmouth and Plymouth in Devon. Here, its pilots were to refuel, be briefed for the mission, and join the other two squadrons flying it, 401 and 412 (Canadian). On the flight down to Bolt Head, the weather was bad and getting worse, threatening the impending mission.

Without McColpin's discipline, the pilots of 133 were overly casual in preparing for Morlaix. Most didn't bother to attend the briefing. Only Brettell and one other pilot were briefed for the raid. In it the met officer gave a tragically erroneous bit of information—a predicted thirty-five-knot headwind at the mission height of 28,000 feet. Further, no one knew precisely when the bombers were to take off, or their precise rendezvous time with the fighters. The pilots lounged under the wings of their

Captain Don Gentile and Captain John Godfrey flew their Mustangs as leader and wingman respectively in combat with the 4th Fighter Group. Captain Gentile: "To show how a team works even when a big brawl has boiled the team down to two men flying wing on each other, Johnny and I spent twenty minutes over Berlin on March 8th and came out of there with six planes destroyed to our credit. I got a straggler, and Johnny got one, and then I got another one fast. A Hun tried to out-turn me, and this was a mistake on his part. Not only can a Messerschmitt 109 not out-turn a Mustang in the upstairs air, but even if he had succeeded, there was Johnny back from his kill and sitting on my tail waiting to shoot him down. He was waiting too, to knock down anybody who tried to bounce me off my kill.

"There were Huns all around. Berlin's air was cloudy with them. The gyrations this dying Hun was making forced me to violent action, but Johnny rode right along like a blocking back who could run with the best. After two Huns had blown up and another had bailed out, Johnny and I formed up tight and went against a team of two Messerschmitts. 'I'll take the port one and you take the starboard one,' I told Johnny, and we came in line abreast and in a two-second burst finished off both of them. They were dead before they knew we were there.

"Then a Messerschmitt bounced Johnny. Johnny turned into him and I swung around to run interference for him. The Hun made a tight swing to get on Johnny's tail, saw me and rolled right under me before I could get a shot in. I rolled with him and fastened to his tail, but by that time we were very close to flak coming up from the city. The Hun wasn't so worried about the flak. I was his immediate and more desperate woe, but flak wasn't my idea of cake to eat, and I didn't dare go slow in it while the Hun took a chance and put his flaps down to slow to a crawl.

"Then I got strikes on him. Glycol started coming out of him, and I had to pass him. But Johnny had fallen into formation right on my wing and he took up the shooting where I had left off. He put more bullets into the Hun while I was swinging up and around to run interference for him. Then he said his ammunition had run out and I said, 'Okay, I'll finish him.' And I followed the Nazi down into the streets clobbering him until he pulled up and bailed out."

American Eagle Squadron members Art Roscoe, above, Jim Gray, above right., and Carroll "Red" McColpin, right; left: The Eagle Squadrons memorial in Grosvenor Square, London.

Captain Don Gentile, right, and below with his P-51 Mustang figthter; right: Captain and Mrs. Gentile.

Spitfires and waited. McColpin's key word, "planning," certainly did not apply. The takeoff was a mess. There were near collisions; pilots didn't get proper instructions about radio channels; some even left maps and escape kits behind.

Flying with auxiliary fuel tanks, thirty-six Spitfires headed out to meet the bombers. There was no sign of them, and the fighters continued on course and called by radio for news of the big friends. The predicted thirty-five-knot headwind had been a major miscalculation. Both bombers and fighters—miles apart— were being whisked along by a one-hundred-knot tailwind. One of the pilots later commented, "It all added up to a streaking catastrophe." Miles ahead of the fighters, the bombers had unknowingly crossed the Bay of Biscay above a blanket of cloud and, on reaching the Pyrenees mountains, discovered their problem, dumped their bombs, and swung back to the north on a reciprocal course, meeting the Spitfires head-on. The fighters turned north as well. By this time all of the aircraft had vanished from the radar plots in England, and communications between bombers, fighters, and their various bases was a shambles. Having been airborne for two hours and fifteen minutes, the Spitfire pilots believed they were near home again and began to let down through the cloud cover. A coastline appeared which they assumed to be England. It was, in fact, the French coast, and they passed over Brest harbor and through a massive flak barrage. In moments, ten Spitfires were lost, four pilots killed and six downed and captured, among them the CO, Gordon Brettell. Two other Spitfires failed to return to Bolt Head. Morlaix was a most unfortunate final mission for the Eagles.

Twice Debden had been the headquarters of 71 (Eagle) Squadron and, on September 29, 1942, it became the base of the newly-formed 4th Fighter Group, Eighth USAAF. The 4th was made up of the three former Eagle Squadrons. In the presence of Major General Carl Spaatz and Air Chief Marshal Sir Sholto Douglas, the Union Jack was hauled down and the Stars and Stripes run up. Sholto Douglas, who had expressed reservations about them in the beginning, had only praise for the transferring American pilots.

"We at Fighter Command deeply regret this parting. In the course of the past eighteen months we have seen the stuff of which you are made. We could not ask for better companions with whom to see this fight through to a finish. Of those who died, those sons of the United States were the first to give their lives for their country. Like their fathers who fought and died with the Lafayette Squadron, so will these Eagles who fell in combat ever remain the honored dead of two great nations."

So parted the Eagles and the RAF. It had not always been a comfortable relationship, but it had laid foundations for Anglo-American cooperation in air fighting, had seen seventy-three enemy aircraft destroyed and hatched the 4th Fighter Group of the Eighth Air Force. The 4th at Debden became the highest-scoring fighter group in the USAAF. A German propaganda statement called the pilots of the group the "Debden Gangsters."

The Eagles are still remembered by the British. A returning veteran was surprised to get a free taxi ride when visiting London in recent years. He asked why. Back came the driver's answer: "You were an Eagle. You already paid."

left and above: Captain Don Gentile
at the Debden base.

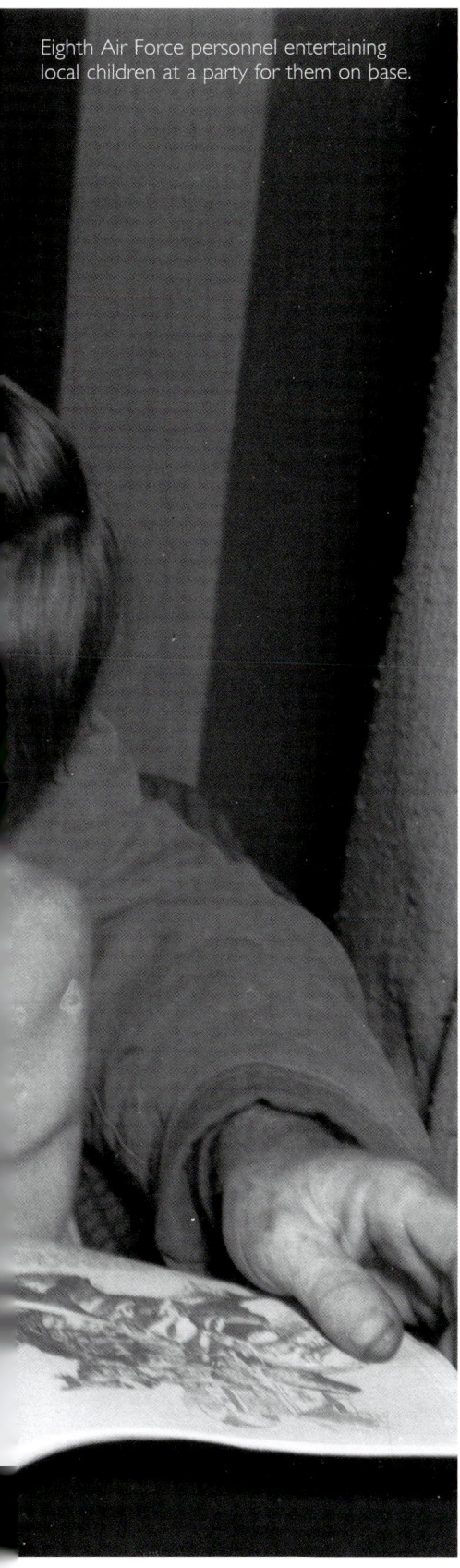

Eighth Air Force personnel entertaining local children at a party for them on base.

You see them in the "local" anywhere in town or country near a fighter station. In flying boots and scarves—their ruffled hair like schoolboys out for a jolly celebration: eight in a car for four had raced along and miracles were wrought to bring them here. To pass an hour with banter, darts and song and drink a pint of two of English beer, and talk of "binds" and "dims" with lots of natter of "ropey jobs" and "wizard types" and "gen" amid much laughter glasses chink and clatter. Deep underneath was hid the real men, who saw their comrades fall out of the skies, and knew too well the look in dead men's eyes.
—*In the Local* by W. A. G. Kemp

"WE WON'T SAY VERY MUCH until we've done something. We hope that after we've gone, you'll be glad we were here." So said Eighth Air Force Lieutenant General Ira Eaker to the British people. Seventy-five years later, the gratitude of the villagers who lived alongside the American airmen and their airfields is still evident. Today, many memorials have been erected on or near the sites of former U.S. air bases in England.

Until war brought a different style of life, Bottisham was a sleepy rural village in the East Anglian countryside. For Bottisham and its neighboring communities of Little Wilbraham and Swaffam Bulbeck, the most exciting local event previously had been the village fete. That was about to change abruptly. So it was for scores of other East Anglian villages when the American invasion came. At Bottisham, though, there was a special relationship between villagers and airmen; a relationship that, since the war, has been strengthened and cherished on both sides of the Atlantic. In part, this can be attributed to the location of the main airfield domestic site within the village itself. Nissen and Maycrete huts were side by side with village houses.

As Station 374, Bottisham became home for the 361st Fighter Group, USAAF, on November 30, 1943. Before that it had been an RAF fighter station. The villagers had become accustomed to aircraft and the eccentricities of those who flew them by the time the Americans arrived. Gone were many acres of farmland. Well-used country lanes were cut and closed. Properties were requisitioned for military use.

Just down the road from the airfield, Bottisham Hall had been home to the Jenyns family for generations. Realizing its potential desirability to the War Office, the Jenyns wisely offered their home for military use before it was taken from them. In return for this patriotic gesture, the family was rewarded with official approval for one elderly member to remain in residence in one of the wings. What Grandma Jenyns thought of the often rowdy activities of her housemates is not recorded. She shared Bottisham Hall with the 361st who made it their Officers' Mess. Surprisingly, when handed back to the family after the war, the house was still in good shape with no significant damage. Only two small broken portions of marble fireplace remind one of the American occupancy. As the officers had stood by the fire drinking and smoking, they discovered that smooth marble was useless for striking a match. The simple solution was to chip off bits of the mantel to provide a rough surface. Outside the house there is further evidence: a moldering squash court, grassed-over foundations of hutted encampments and faded traces of white "blackout" bands painted on trees in the driveway. Other nearby trees bear carvings:

WALT-WISCONSIN and EMILY AND JACK 1944 are messages from the past. Elsewhere in the village, traces of Eighth Air Force wall art have survived until recently in the Maycrete huts and have been preserved for museums: a GI astride the cowling of a Thunderbolt, the Statue of Liberty, a flying tractor, and a transatlantic liner. And plenty of stories still abound.

Jack Heath, then a farm laborer in his mid-twenties, witnessed the airfield activity from Frog End Farm. Jack liked to spend his leisure time in the local pubs, where he got to know several of the Yanks. He remembered Cookie, Big Finn, and Mexican Pete, who, with their fellow airmen, frequented the Hole in the Wall, the Greyhound, the Carpenter's Arms, the King's Head, and the Swan. Over pints of Greene King, the villagers rubbed shoulders with the Americans. The company of these colorful Yanks could be a pleasure, but when they were full of beer, not always so. "Old Pete," recalled Jack, "was a big, unpleasant chap with a pockmarked and sallow complexion. And, with a few pints inside him he became even more unpleasant and always ready for a fight. One evening I was riding home on my bike and he came at me from behind with a bottle. Wallop! He

landed me one and sent me over the handlebars onto the road. Then he set about my mate and cut him over his eye. Suddenly, he dropped the bottle and it rolled toward me. Right, I thought, now it's your turn. But just then two other Yanks turned up and restrained him."

Pubs were the center of village social life and since there was no other local entertainment, it was natural that the Americans would patronize them. Many of the villagers' memories are associated with times spent drinking with the GIs. At the Carpenter's Arms, landlord Tom Middleditch and his wife, Gertie, welcomed the young airmen warmly. Big Finn took advantage of Middleditch's hospitality and, in a memorable binge, drank thirty-two pints of beer—eighteen in a morning session and a further fourteen during the evening. This impressed the folk of Bottisham and led to one of the Yanks offering an inviting challenge to Jack and his pals: "We're gonna teach you Limeys how to really drink!" "Well," Jack replied, "if you've got the money, we've got the time."

Not all English villagers, though, remember things being quite so convivial between them and their American visitors. Cecil Savage of

English children are shown an American B-17 bomber during a party for them at the 379th Bomb Group base, Kimbolton, October 1943.

Steeple Morden, home to the 355th Fighter Group, recalled: "Of all the bombs they dropped, they should have dropped one here in the center of Steeple Morden. They make all this fuss about memorials and the like, but it weren't like that then. Oh no. Most of the people here were quite unfriendly to the American boys. At least, that's my impression. Why, they wouldn't even open the church, village hall or the like for the boys to go sit and relax in their time off. Just down at Litlington, though, I remember it was a different story. The lads seemed welcome there. The Congregational church was opened up for them whenever they wanted, but Steeple Morden? No. Do you know, the ladies in the village were even afraid to talk to the lads for fear of what others might say, and if any of them had invited the American boys in for tea, well, they'd be accused of being loose. The gossip would soon get around that so-and so had had a Yank in her house and that she must be after some nylons."

If some Steeple Morden residents could be accused of a coldness bordering on hostility to the Yanks, they at least could not be accused of the savagery of some of the American Military Police to their fellow servicemen, as witnessed by Cecil. "Oh, they had wickedly long truncheons and beat the Yank airmen absolutely mercilessly when they rounded them up from the pubs at closing time. It was all quite unnecessary. Once, and I saw this myself, an MP pulled his pistol and shot one of the poor boys in the leg—as if he were a rabbit—just because he tried to run off."

War brings out the best and worst in human nature, civilian and military, and it is easy to imagine the upheaval and resentment that ensued when both groups were

brought together. Often the passage of time filters out unpleasant memories, leaving the happier ones. But whether memories are good or bad, it remains that the local population played an important part in the lives of the U.S. servicemen, who in turn brought some color to the austere wartime lives of their hosts.

Jock Wells and his pals rushed from school each day to watch the American planes up at the Bottisham base. Apart from the thrill of seeing the aircraft take off and land, there was the added attraction of candy and gum. "Us lads knew where all the local chickens would lay their eggs, so we regularly collected them and took them to the airfield. One of the dispersal points was up against a lane and the Americans would pass a long telescopic pole through the coiled barbed wire. On the end was a net and we'd put the eggs in it, and in return would come back a net full of candy and gum."

Memories of exciting crash landings . . . of a GI shooting rats on the blister hangar roof . . . of the locals scavenging for food in the Americans' rubbish pit . . . and of the weekly dances endure for Jock and others from Bottisham and the neighboring villages. "They were mostly happy times for us, but on one occasion the reality of war came home. We had 'adopted' a particular pilot called Geigerson and his fighter—a Thunderbolt named *Contrary Mary*. We used to wait for him to come back, but one day he didn't. Just after D-Day he was lost shooting up a flak train, but the memory of him standing on the wing of his plane, emptying his pockets of candy after a mission and throwing it across the wire to us kids will always be with me."

Jack Heath remembered a head-on collision between a Mustang and

a Thunderbolt near the airfield. He recalled seeing the flaming wreckage falling into a cornfield, setting the standing corn alight, and the panic as he and the other farm workers struggled to save their valuable Allis-Chalmers combine harvester from the burning crop. More important, men they had known and befriended had died violently and horribly as they watched. Usually death was more remote than that. Pilots and aircraft simply didn't come back—as if they had flown off to another place.

There were other losses. In all, the 361st lost eighty-one aircraft during its time in the European theater, including that of its highly respected commanding officer, Colonel Thomas Christian, who was posted missing in action after a strafing attack on August 12, 1944. After he had left his home in Texas for England, his young wife bore him a daughter, Lou, whom he would never see. He named all of his fighters after her. At Bottisham Hall, Colonel Christian had shared a room with his old friend and deputy commander of

left: Bottisham resident Jack Heath; overleaf: Patrons of the Woodman Inn—wartime home of the 55th Fighter Group and, later, the 398th Bomb Group—chatting with Eighth Air Force ground personnel from the base. The 55th operated P-38 Lightning fighters from the field. The Woodman was only a short hike from the runways of the Nuthampstead base.

the 361st, Joseph Kruzel. Writing to Lou of her father, in later years, Kruzel recalled: "The friendship and high regard I held him in grew even deeper as we worked together to assemble the group and prepare it for combat. When we got to Bottisham he and I shared thoughts about our loved ones back home. He wanted so much to see you. We shared, too, the excitement and sad times which go along with wars, but I got to know a man who was an absolutely outstanding leader and as concerned about his enlisted

men as he was his officers. He also appreciated the importance of maintaining good relations with the local community and, in my view, managed to do so. I saw in him a sense of confidence, discipline, fairness and maturity you rarely see in a man of twenty-seven. Had he survived the war, he would, I am convinced, have become one of the U.S. Air Force's outstanding leaders. He was, to me, four-star general officer material."

The qualities that Kruzel recognized in Thomas Christian were remem-

bered with admiration by many in the local population around Bottisham. In 1988, a company called Bellway Homes developed the former communal site of the 361st into a new residential area and joined with the villagers in naming a road there Thomas Christian Way. Beside the road a memorial was erected and dedicated in his honor.

In an emotional pilgrimage to Bottisham to unveil the memorial to the father she had never known, Lou Christian Wilson Fleming experienced

together barely eight months before the war took Christian away. Among the relics of her late father was a letter posted to Bottisham on August 11, the day before his death. "Sorry to hear about your backing into the painter's car. How is the old jalopy (oops!) holding out? Did you ever get any more tires? What are the prospects of a new one after I get back? Are they still making them? What models, etc?

"Golly, doesn't Lou have to have something to 'chew' on now—or does she still work on that thumb? If so, maybe you should break her of it—shouldn't you? I'm glad you're not giving in to her when she cries for attention (but I'll bet you do lots of times). She has got to be disciplined tho. It probably was just her tooth bothering her.

"Yes, darling, our love is the 'forever and ever' variety and it's not a bunch of nonsense. It just is. I may not be able to say it as romantically fifty years from now as I have tried all these past five years, but it will always be in my heart that way. It's the perfect completeness of it that continually inspires me. So very few things are complete when you stop to think about it."

The letters, the pilgrimage, the memorial and, above all, the villagers helped Lou come to terms with grieving for her father—"a sad but necessary experience." After the dedication ceremony she commented: "It's a poignant moment and I have learned more and feel closer to my father now than I ever have." As the Mustang flew overhead she added: "It's an unforgettable experience. I feel like my father is flying that plane and I feel so close to him and to the village of Bottisham."

You must look into the people as well as at them.
—Chesterfield

Lou Christian, the daughter of Colonel Thomas Christian, commanding officer of the 361st Fighter Group, Bottisham, England.

With vacant stare in the market square, decked out in a lilac suit, the villager stands with great hands and chaffs with a raw recruit. The heat comes down on a sleepy town like a blanket over the head, and a church clock beats in the silent streets saying "Dead, dead, dead." The hour of seven is just like heaven, the moment of wishful drinking! Giggling wenches on bar-room benches can guess what the boys are thinking. Shropshire lads look a bunch of cads as they jingle the week-end cash, and girls on munitions in certain conditions regret they were once so rash.
—from *Rural Sunday* by Michael Barsley

In this world a man must either be anvil or hammer.
—from *Hyperion* by Longfellow

the same warmth and friendship the villagers had shown her father forty-four years earlier. It was a deeply moving ceremony for Lou, especially when a Mustang roared low overhead in salute. Until that visit she had known little of her father. All her mother had told her had been "he was a hero . . . a good man . . . he would have been proud of you."

Until her trip, Lou had been unable to bring herself to read through a trunk full of letters written by her parents to each other. They had been

below: Local children enjoying the hospitality of the 379th Bomb Group at their Kimbolton, England base; top right: Colonel and Mrs. Thomas Christian when he was in command of the 361st Fighter Group at Bottisham; bottom right: The officers' quarters of the 361st Fighter Group, Bottisham Hall.

IN THE BEGINNING

A still from the 1941 film *I Wanted Wings* starring William Holden and Ray Milland.

THE DAYLIGHT ATTACKS by RAF Bomber Command in the early years of the war had been no more than token forays. At night, though, its bombers had been raiding targets in Germany as well as northern Italy, and during the Battle of Britain it had pounded the assembling German invasion fleets in France. From the outset of the war, the RAF had seemed more comfortable with night operations. Its daytime raids on targets just inside France and Belgium drew heavily on the resources of RAF Fighter Command. The bomber formations escorted by Hurricanes and Spitfires of 11 Group on what the RAF called "Circuses" were often costly exercises. These were the early days of protective fighter escort.

On April 16, 1941, a mission was launched by Blenheims of 21 Squadron against the heavily defended Luftwaffe fighter field at Berck-sur-Mer. Their escort was made up of 601 Squadron Hurricanes and 303 (Polish) Squadron Spitfires. The Spitfires provided top cover while the Hurricanes flew close escort. Outbound, the flight was uneventful although a formation of Messerschmitt ME 109s was observed at higher altitude. The forces did not engage in combat.

Delivering their bombs on target, and damaging or destroying seven of the new ME 109Fs on the ground, the Blenheims turned for home with their escort, unhindered by flak or enemy fighters; their return across the Channel was also without incident until they reached the English coast at Dungeness. With the advantages of height and sun, a formation of 109s of Werner Mölders' JG 53 tore through the British fighters, with cannon and machine guns blazing. The weavers, flying to protect the rear of the RAF formation, were the first to be picked off. Two of the Polish airmen were

shot down. Pilot Officer Waskiewicz was hit and sent plunging into the Channel while Pilot Officer Mierzwa's Spitfire exploded on the pebbled beach near Dungeness lighthouse.

The RAF pilots broke in all directions. Wing Commander "Minnie" Manton, who had recently been appointed to oversee operations such as this one, was having an unfortunate indoctrination. Wounded, and with his Hurricane badly holed, he prepared to bail out. The Luftwaffe had even removed the hood for him. But then a glance at the sea made him reconsider. The airplane did seem controllable. With enough altitude to glide back across the coast, he would try to put the battered kite down somewhere. He had spun down from the combat area and a quick check confirmed that no one was on his tail. He managed to get the Hurricane down in a farmer's field and was lucky to survive as the aircraft cartwheeled across a drainage ditch and tore itself apart. His Sutton seat harness had been damaged in the attack and Manton was pitched forward and knocked unconscious. A gashed forehead, shrapnel wounds, severe bruising, and a chipped spine were to keep him off ops for some time.

The rest of 601 Squadron was having a hard time too. Its commanding officer, Squadron Leader John "Peggy" O'Neill, was hit and forced to bail out into the sea. Whitney Straight, an American pilot in 601, circled overhead to guide rescue boats to O'Neill's dinghy in Rye Bay. As O'Neill was being rescued, Group Captain Thomas McEvoy, station commander of 601 and 303's Northolt base, was crash-landing his damaged Hurricane on the Dungeness beach. McEvoy was not an operational pilot and had just come along to observe.

As suddenly as they had come the

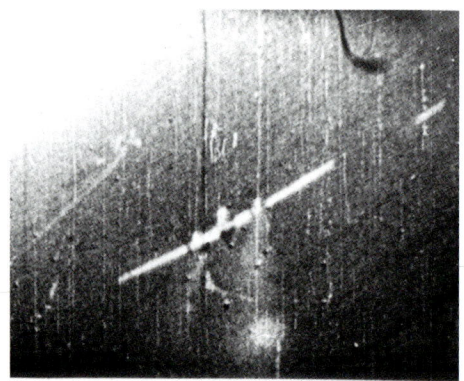

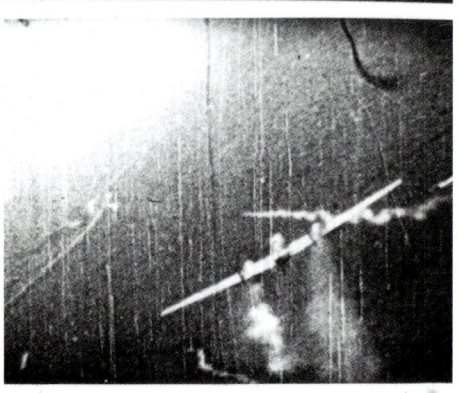

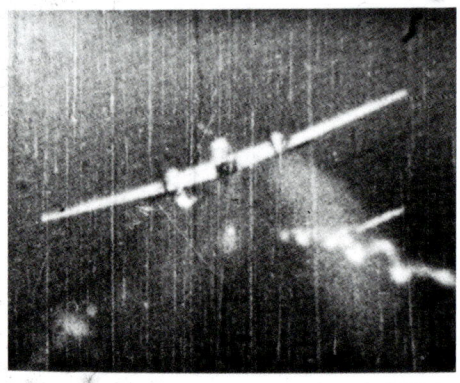

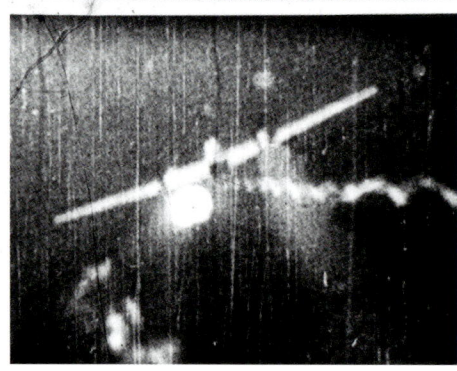

above: Gun camera footage of the downing of a German aircraft; right: Residents of Ponders End, Enfield, with the wreckage of a Bf 110 shot down in their gardens on August 30, 1940.

Messerschmitts disappeared, leaving behind two dead and four wounded RAF pilots, and five aircraft destroyed, for no loss of their own. "They slized us to beets," said a wounded Pilot Officer Strembosz on returning to Northolt in his crippled Spitfire.

The British bombers had escaped the attack without loss and the results of their bombing on Berck-sur-Mer had been good, even though the operation had been a disaster for their fighter escorts. However, a lesson had been learned about fighter escort tactics from this debacle. Having the fighters tied so closely to the bombers was a mistake, and flying fighter squadrons in archaic "air display" formations was suicidal. And finally, the need was recognized for effective rear-cover fighter protection for returning bomber formations whose escorts were low on fuel. But the value of the Circus missions that pioneered the fighter-escorted daylight bombing raids into occupied Europe was questionable. The cost in bombers, fighters, and crews was unacceptable in relation to the limited success of these escort missions.

Neville Duke, later to achieve fame as a test pilot and holder of the world air speed record, had just joined 92 Squadron at Biggin Hill when the Circus missions began. He recalled: "Stirling bombers were being used for these daylight raids, usually flying, in threes with Spitfires for escorts. On one occasion, though, 92 Squadron provided top cover for nine Blenheims which were bombing Hazebrouck marshaling yards. I was glad, and a bit relieved, when I got down again after this show. We were at 25,000 feet and there were a lot of 109s about. One of them managed to latch onto my tail and suddenly I saw tracer going over my hood. I was able to get out of his way by turning hard

and climbing—only to be jumped by eight more of his friends. I used all the dodges I could think of, but only managed to get away from them when I was well out to sea. To add insult to injury I was then attacked by a Spitfire . . . fortunately without result."

The next time out, Duke got a confirmed ME 109 kill in a dogfight over the Channel between Dover and Calais. In the twisting maneuvers he became disoriented and was climbing while inverted, unable to distinguish between the blue of the sea and that of the sky. Then a 109 was framed in his gunsight; he fired and the German went into a slow spin toward the sea . . . and Duke was reoriented. By the end of that day he had been on ops three times.

In the next year the escort operations of RAF Fighter Command produced mixed results. One pilot commented: "Circuses? They were never half so much fun as any circus I had ever been to, but whoever dreamed up the idea was certainly a clown!" The RAF was paying a heavy price in its new offensive role, including the deaths of the outstanding fighter leaders Brendan "Paddy" Finucane and Victor Beamish, and the loss of the legless legend, Douglas Bader, boss of the Tangmere Wing. As a young man in 1931, Bader had been involved in a flying accident that resulted in the amputation of both his legs.

Shot down over France on August 9, 1941, Bader was fortunate to survive. One of his artificial legs had become lodged in the damaged cockpit of his fighter, trapping him. Finally, he managed to break free of the prosthesis and bail out safely, but into captivity. "Buck" Casson was flying with 616 Squadron of the Tangmere wing under Bader's command, and he too was shot down and captured that day. Casson recalled: "On this

Blind Date, a high-time B-17 Flying Fortress
bomber of the 388th Bomb Group at Knettishall,
England, in May 1944.

operation it was a novel experience for us to have ample height for attack, instead of being in the role of underdog." But despite this advantage, Casson and Bader were downed by Adolf Galland and his formidable JG 26 wing. Galland's admiration of Bader led him to ask Reichsmarshall Hermann Goering for permission to contact the Royal Air Force to request that a spare set of prosthetic legs be dropped by parachute near Galland's French base. Radio contact was made with the RAF on an international SOS wavelength and the English were informed of Bader's capture and the request for his artificial limbs was made. Shortly thereafter, Galland's base and other targets in the St. Omer area were bombed by the RAF, who later notified Galland's unit that, in addition to bombs, they had dropped the requested spare legs. The Germans then located a large box near their airfield. The box had been painted with a red cross and German lettering: THIS BOX CONTAINS ARTIFICIAL LEGS FOR WING COMMANDER BADER, PRISONER OF WAR. When taken into German custody at Galland's St. Omer base, Casson was informed that Bader was also a prisoner. Refusing to acknowledge that he knew Bader, Casson would only admit to having heard of him in the service. "Quite honestly, I just couldn't believe it. Neither could anyone else in Fighter Command."

A year later, on August 19, 1942, at Dieppe, RAF fighter units fought hard and well in the famous raid, but more significantly, fighter units of the U.S. Eighth Air Force saw action in the ETO for the first time. It marked the beginning of an illustrious campaign.

From the start of American air operations in England, "Monk" Hunter, commanding general of VIII Fighter Command, was hampered by the limited operating range of his aircraft. Assigned to accompany the Eighth's B-17 and B-24 bombers then being organized for deep-penetration raids into Germany, his then-current fighters carried insufficient fuel to cover such distances. The early Spitfires with which the first 8AF fighter groups were equipped couldn't do the job, nor could the new Thunderbolts or the early Mustangs. Even the innovative P-38 Lightning was incapable of such long hauls. What the bombers required was total fighter protection, all the way there and all the way back.

At Bovingdon, near London, the technical experts of Eighth Fighter Command were working on a system of long-range drop tanks for the fighters. Different types were tried, including resinated paper 205-gallon tanks and metal tanks that could be pressurized. Technical snags, shortages, and slow delivery from the United States caused a delay of several months before drop tanks were available in quantity for the Thunderbolt. It was not until mid-summer of 1943 that drop tanks became standard operational equipment, extending the fighter radius of action by about eighty miles. The concept called for the fighters to use the fuel in their external tanks first, then dump the empty containers. The ungainly pods would consequently no longer inhibit the performance of the fighter in combat. The fighters' range would be extended further in time, and ultimately, the ultra-long-range P-51D Mustang would become available in large numbers; but for the time being the escort capability was to be a narrow one.

The American fighters took their bombers as far as they could until forced to withdraw, usually somewhere near the Dutch-German border. Flak, the weather and enemy fighters continually threatened the

bombers and their escort. Aware of the fuel limitations of the 8AF fighter escorts, the German interceptors often shadowed the massive American formations, waiting for the moment when the escorting fighters would have to turn for home and the bombers were left untended and alone. At this point in the war, the main German fighter units were still well equipped, well organized, well led—and determined.

The Americans soon realized that the defensive firepower of the bomber formations would not, in itself, protect them. Close fighter escort from home base to target and back was the only way to operate. Newly-arrived P-38 Lightnings soon demonstrated their superior range to that of the drop tank–fitted P-47 Thunderbolts that then equipped most 8AF fighter units. On November 13, 1943, the Lightnings escorted a force of B-24s to Bremen. In a fierce air battle, the 48th Fighter Squadron of the 14th Fighter Group shot down several German fighters. Though other American fighter groups lost seven P-38s on this mission, not a single

B-24 was lost to enemy fighters. The point had been made. If our fighters could stick with the bombers all the way, our losses to enemy fighters could be minimized.

Long before the range problem was resolved, American bombers were being sent to attack targets deep in Germany and were incurring intolerable losses. As the bomber force struggled back from the target area to fighter-escort range where the rear cover wing of Thunderbolts or Lightnings would pick them up, the sight of these "Little Friends" was as welcome as the longed-for first glimpse of the English coastline.

"Hub" Zemke's 56th Fighter Group, the Wolfpack, was one of the outfits assigned to escort duty in

Among the most famous of the RAF fighter pilots in the Second World War were Douglas Bader, at left, and James "Ginger" Lacey. They are seen here together visiting a film set during the making of *Battle of Britain* in 1968; far left and far right, wartime portraits by Cuthbert Orde of Bader and Lacey, respectively.

left: Hubert "Hub" Zemke commanded the Thunderbolt pilots of the 56th Fighter Group at Boxted and Halesworth. The 56th was one of the Eighth Air Force's highest-scoring fighter groups of the war; below: A Republic P-47 Thunderbolt escorting 8AF bombers on a mission to a German target in 1943.

the early days of the mass daylight bombing raids. One of Zemke's pilots, Walker "Bud" Mahurin, recalled that altitude, as well as range, was a vital consideration to the Thunderbolt pilots: "At heights above 30,000 feet the P-47 could outturn and outrun any Messerschmitt 109. Below that, it was still a pretty good match, but its rate of climb was less than impressive. Conscious of the critical altitude factor, and in a belief that less weight equaled more altitude and a better climbing performance, Zemke once stripped out of his P-47 every item of equipment he considered superfluous—the armor plating, bullet-proof windscreen . . . even the relief tube. When he had finished, the revetment where his airplane was parked looked like a junkyard. With his new 'light-weight' P-47, he led the 56th on another escort mission. Over German-held territory, he had a scare. A .50 caliber bullet slammed into his

cockpit, entering where the armored windscreen had previously been. It narrowly missed his head and tore through the back of the cockpit. The bullet had been fired by a B-17 gunner testing his weapon. Back on the ground Zemke put all the junk back on his airplane again."

In the late summer of 1943, a force of B-17s raided Münster and discovered to its cost what could happen if a planned fighter shield was not in place. Fighter cover had been intended and was to be provided (in fact, by the Wolfpack) but a slight navigational error en route made the Thunderbolts late for their rendezvous with the bombers. Catastrophe resulted for the lead bomber wing, comprising the 100th, 95th, and 390th Bomb Groups. In minutes the 100th was almost completely destroyed; half of the 390th was shot down, as was a quarter of the 95th. Twenty-nine B-17s were lost—nearly all of them

to German fighters. In human terms, the loss equalled two-thirds of the casualties suffered by RAF Fighter Command in the Battle of Britain—but this time the losses had been inflicted in a matter of minutes. With adequate fighter protection these losses would certainly have been fewer. Clearly, the attrition rate of the American bombers was unacceptable and could not be tolerated regardless of bombing results.

top left and center: P-47s of the 56th Fighter Group; top right: A Messerschmitt Bf 109 down on a beach in northern France; left: B-17Fs releasing their bombs on a German target in 1943.

DISTRACTIONS

English girls entertained at a party on an
American air base in England during 1944.

IT WASN'T ALL BLOODSHED, boredom, and booze. There were . . . distractions. In one form or another, the female of the species featured as prominently in the life of the fighter pilot as the airplane in which he went to war. Pinup or wife, sweetheart or mother figure, all played a part in boosting morale and normalizing an otherwise abnormal existence.

Unlike other experiences of war, the memories of those girls remain mostly pleasant. Apart from the wives and sweethearts though, the image of one girl persists with many American and British servicemen: Jane, the comic-strip cutie. Along with Betty Grable and Vera Lynn, she ranks as one of the best-loved girls of the war years, especially among the fliers.

Jane was everybody's girlfriend. She was leggy, curvaceous, a scatterbrain . . . and a sensation. She oozed sex appeal—yet was naively unaware of it. In fact, she was a fantasy girl, the creation of cartoonist Norman Pett, and she appeared nearly every day in the London *Daily Mirror*. Readers invariably turned to see Jane's capers before scanning the news. The headlines could wait. What had Jane been up to? No wonder one member of Parliament referred to the Allied Forces, in a House of Commons speech, as "Jane's Fighting Men." Her success was astounding, yet the storyline was entirely predictable. She would always lose her scanty clothes, or most of them, in this particular comic strip.

The model for Norman Pett's Jane was, in fact, Chrystabel Leighton-Porter, an attractive and vivacious young blonde. Given the success of the cartoon, there was a demand for Jane to appear in person and a stage show was conceived. It was considered to be quite risqué, but despite complaints from those who

safeguarded public morals, the shows were put on almost daily in theaters around Britain. Her "act" was portrayed through windows positioned across the stage to suggest the boxes of her comic strip. The audience saw Jane and her little dachshund Fritz as shadows against a white screen.

With the rationing and shortages of wartime Britain, pretty clothes were hard to find, an ironic problem for a girl best known for her state of undress. Her creator's frequent failure to meet his newspaper deadline, however, ensured that Jane was never short of one item. Pett's tardiness with the artwork caused the *Daily Mirror* to threaten to drop the series, which they eventually did. There was such an outcry that the cartoon was immediately brought back, its absence explained in a single drawing of a flustered Jane and the words: "Give me a break, boys. I've lost my panties!" The reaction was swift and overwhelming. The offices of the *Mirror* were deluged with undies.

At the height of the Blitz bombing, Jane was putting on nightly shows in London. The servicemen loved them and flocked to each performance. Every night as she concluded her show she would invite a male in the audience to join her on stage in a song-and-dance routine. Often he would be an American airman. Both Jane and her real-life model, Chrystabel . . . had a special affection for Americans. "They were wonderful. So full of life and so much fun. In fact, the Yanks fell in love with England . . . with English girls . . . and with me," Chrystabel remembered. Many proposed to her.

It was an RAF fighter pilot, however, whose proposal she eventually accepted: Flying Officer Arthur Leighton-Porter, who flew Typhoons in 182 Squadron. But the marriage

An American Red Cross girl greets airmen on their return from a mission.

was a hush-hush affair. Her image as a pinup and as "everyone's girl" would have been shattered had news of the marriage leaked. Consequently, her wedding became one of the best-kept secrets of the war. Jane's eventual postwar "marriage" to the character Georgie Porgie when the cartoon series ended caused an uproar and even made the BBC news.

Chrystabel recalled that the well-heeled American fighter pilots were a great hit with the girls in Jane's theater company. "Some of them would get our tour dates and follow us around the country to all the different venues in one great gang. After the show they'd have taxis lined up to take us on to a club, or for a meal and some music and dancing. In London it would be the Savoy, where they had made a basement ballroom safe from the bombs falling above as we danced."

When they had bribed the band-leader to play "As Time Goes By" for the last time, it was taxis home for Chrystabel and her girls to which-ever hotel happened to be "home" for that week. But like thousands of other wives in wartime, she had to get on with life aware that her hus-band was in constant danger. And, since the marriage had to be kept a secret, she couldn't confide in anyone about Arthur. The moments they could spend together were few. Their leaves rarely coincided and wartime travel was difficult. On-base visits by wives and girlfriends were not encour-aged by RAF station commanders. As Major James Goodson of the U.S. 4th Fighter Group put it: "Marriage tempered a man too much and the cautious pilot is doomed. I've never seen a fighter pilot marry and keep on the way he was. He gets careful, thinking about his wife. The first thing you know he's thinking about her and a Hun bounces his tail."

There were, of course, other girls in the lives of the fighter pilots, and a special one in the life of Harley Brown of the Kings Cliffe–based 20th Fighter Group, USAAF.

The excitement and novelty of being in a strange country and flying fighters was matched by only one thing: the English girls. With so many of the English servicemen away at war, the coast was clear for the American pilots, who moved in with gusto. They brought an easy-going and flattering breeziness to the art of dating. These Yanks were really something. What British serviceman could compete with the money, the accent, the uni-form? Descending on the cities, towns, and villages of Britain, the Americans launched an attack with candy, nylons, nail polish, and perfume. It was called "shack-up material" and, while such aids to conquest were not always suc-cessful, the young American service-man was rarely offended or discour-aged by a firm refusal. There was sure to be some other honey anxious for his attentions. But Harley Brown need-ed neither money, perfume, nylons, nor accent to win his girl. It was just plain old-fashioned love at first sight.

On leave from their first base at Goxhill, Brown and two friends had crossed the River Humber for a day out in Hull. There, they went to a typically English tea room for refresh-ment. "We were standing there wait-ing for an empty table when I noticed two English girls dressed in the National Fire Service uniforms hav-ing their tea and crumpets. One was a brunette and the other the most beautiful blonde I had ever seen. I told my two buddies, the heck with waiting for an empty table. We approached their table and asked if we could join them. What two girls could say no to three handsome young pilots standing there in their new uniforms with the

silver wings and shiny gold bars? While getting acquainted we learned that the girls were telephone operators in the NFS and on their afternoon break. Before they had to go back to work I had gotten the blonde's phone number and address. During the next two weeks, every time I could get a day or even a few hours off, I'd call her and head for Hull."

Harley Brown's blonde was Peggie Blaymires. Their relationship was to survive his subsequent posting south to Kings Cliffe. When the war in Europe ended Harley went back to the United States on three months' rest leave. Although he and Peggie were engaged by this time and had made plans for a wedding, the relationship seemed to be going the way of so many wartime romances between English girls and American servicemen—nowhere. A return to the UK for Harley was now out of the question and Peggie could not get to America. But somehow their relationship lasted. They remained in touch and in love until, in June 1946, Peggie got to New York and the couple was married. Forty-five years later Harley's little Yorkshire lass was still the most beautiful blonde he had ever seen.

It was the girls in the services who figured most immediately in the lives of the Allied fighter pilots. Driver, plotter, clerk, or nurse, the girls in uniform were often more than just that to the fliers. Friendships and romances flourished between the pilots and the girls working together on the same stations.

Edith Heap was only twenty years old when she volunteered to join the Women's Auxiliary Air Force the day after war broke out. Aircraftwoman Heap enlisted as a driver and reported for duty at RAF Yeadon in her home county of Yorkshire. Posted later to Debden in Essex, she drove trucks and tractors, and laid out flare paths for the Hurricane fighters at the RAF station. She enjoyed her work. "We were all so young and naïve, and although a lot of the boys were knockouts, we hardly knew how to treat the opposite sex because we had all been segregated at school. Holding hands or perhaps a peck on the cheek was enough to send us into ecstasies, and most of what went on was just lighthearted chat and a sort of banter we'd developed to keep the boys in order."

At Debden Edith met twenty-year-old Denis Wissler, a pilot officer on a short-service commission flying Hurricanes with 17 Squadron. By the time of the Battle of Britain she was remustered and had become an operations room plotter, while Denis was in the thick of the fighting. "When the controller had vectored the squadron toward the enemy, we would hear shouts of 'Tally-Ho' over the RT and a running commentary from the pilots. We listened to 'Blue Two going down in flames,' without knowing whether he had managed to bail out.'

On September 24, 1940, Denis was shot down by a Messerschmitt ME 109 over the Thames Estuary. He managed to make it back to Debden, where he crash-landed on the airfield. He was admitted to Saffron Walden Hospital with an arm wound and Edith visited him there frequently. He returned to duty and, shortly after, his squadron was posted away to Martlesham Heath on the Suffolk coast. By this point he and Edith were in love and from then on they wrote to each other every day and met whenever their duties allowed.

They managed to get a twenty-four-hour pass together. "We went to Cambridge, but the Garden House Hotel there was full, except for a

left: Chrystabel Leighton-Porter, the model for Norman Pett's comic strip character, *Jane*; lower left: Kath Preston, wartime proprietor of the White Hart Inn, Brasted, England; right: Edith Heap, a WAAF aorcraft plotter and the fiancé of RAF Pilot Officer Denis Wissler.

double room. Denis came out and told me that he had declined the double room and asked if that was right. I said yes, and wondered later if he would have asked me to marry him if I had said no. We eventually found single rooms at the Red Lion at Trumpington. We had dinner and lots of chat. It was getting late and Denis came to my room and sat on the bed. He asked me to marry him. I said yes of course and he ordered a bottle of champagne, which the manager brought up. I was surprised that he didn't say anything about Denis being in my room, definitely not done in those days. And, after all of the bubbly, we went to our respective beds."

Once they had the approval of Denis's commanding officer and their families, the wedding date was set for January 4. Then came November 11.

Although Denis's squadron had moved to Martlesham Heath, it was still controlled by the ops room at Debden, where Edith was a plotter. "Just before we came off watch at 1200 hours, there was a cry of 'Blue Four going down in the drink.' I was paralyzed with fear. I knew who it was, and I knew what had happened, but I allowed myself to hope. When we left Ops, I didn't bother with lunch, but went up to Motor Transport to talk to old friends. Later, I got the news. Yes, it was true, he

was missing. No parachute observed."

When men like Denis failed to return from a mission, some pilots looked for comfort from mother figures like Kath Preston, landlady of the White Hart at Brasted. The pub was a popular haunt of the Biggin Hill pilots and she had quickly learned to recognize the symptoms of a loss when "her boys" came in. "Sometimes the usual crowd would come in and perhaps they would be a bit subdued. Then you would realize that a face was missing and the best friend of the missing man was sitting alone in the corner, drinking."

In situations like that Kath knew to say nothing. They didn't want to talk

about the missing man. No other subjects were taboo, however, between Kath and her pilot customers. In her mid-thirties, she was a woman of maturity and experience to these very young men. They would take her into their confidence about their problems and their love lives. Kath was always there to listen as a trusted and respected friend. She was fun too. A joke, a kind word, a game of darts, and a four-penny pint of mild beer on the house was her way of entering into the spirit of things. It could not have always been easy for her, though. Her husband Teddy was away in the navy and she feared for his safety—a kind of fear that Jane,

Peggie, and Edith shared.

In her own way Kath was serving her country by cheering Biggin Hill's "Few." She contributed immeasurably to the morale of those pilots. Doubtless there were other Kaths in the lives of the fighter pilots, but none could surpass the warmth, affection and caring of Kath Preston.

Girls, friends, wives, lovers, whoever they may have been, almost every Allied fighter pilot had his often short life enriched by a Jane, an Edith, a Peggie, or a Kath. He needed her.

left: Field canteens operated by the American Red Cross were standard features on the airfields of the Eighth U.S. Army Air Force in WW2 England; above: Girls from the chorus of the famous Windmill Theatre, London, on a visit to the men of the 4th Fighter Group at Debden, Essex, in 1944.

The Wolf Wagon bus used to bring girls from nearby villages to dances and parties at the Leiston base of the 357th Fighter Group.

GIVE US
THE TOOLS

Members of the American
WASPs, the Women
Airforce Service Pilots.

Oh, what a blamed uncertain thing this pesky weather is. It blew and snew and then it thew, and now, by jing, it's friz.
—Philander Johnson

RECKLESS, COLORFUL, EGOTISTICAL, FLASHY, AGGRESSIVE—all descriptives commonly associated with World War II fighter pilots. But there were others, very different types, who flew the Mustangs, Lightnings, Thunderbolts, Spitfires, and Hurricanes in a noncombatant role, out of the limelight. They were the men and women delivery pilots of the Air Transport Auxiliary, the ATA, an organization of which Lord Beaverbrook, Churchill's Minister for Aircraft Production, later said: "They carried out the delivery of aircraft from the factories to the RAF, thus relieving countless numbers of RAF pilots for duty in battle. They were soldiers fighting in the struggle just as completely as if they had been engaged on the battle front."

Petite and attractive Diana Barnato was as far removed from the archetypal battlefront soldier as one could be. Granddaughter of the diamond-mining magnate Barney Barnato and daughter of the famous racing driver Woolfe "Babe" Barnato, she selected war work as a Red Cross Voluntary Aid Detachment, VAD, nurse, a suitably feminine occupation for an ex-debutante. But a chance meeting with the chief flying instructor of the newly-formed ATA, while out riding in Windsor Park, was to change her life.

Diana had learned to fly during 1937 at the Brooklands Flying Club and had soloed after only six hours of lessons. "I really hadn't a clue what I was doing and waggled the stick around as if stirring a pudding. I always remember that I was getting ready to taxi out for my solo and a little man came running over and hung onto the edge of the cockpit staring up at me. He had a hidiously burned and disfigured face, and called out, 'Miss Barnato, please don't fly. Look what it done to me.' Well, I took off anyway although, in fact, he did me a very good turn. Later, whenever I got in a tight spot, I thought of that man and his little face looking up at me. It had been a salutary experience, even though I ignored him at the time.

"After a mere ten hours of flying I couldn't afford it anymore on my own pocket money and had to give up. Later, when I was invited to take a test for the ATA, it seemed my flying experience of a few years before was hardly sufficient qualification, but they said I was 'promising' and asked me to come and have the test anyway."

At that time there were only eight ATA women pilots in the service and, despite the exploits of famed aviators like Amy Johnson and Amelia Earhart, flying was not considered an occupation appropriate for females, least of all in wartime. With that in mind, Diana was not hopeful about passing her test. Then a riding accident delayed her taking the test, and it was a further six months before she took it, passed, and joined up as a trainee pilot. She was taught to fly again, from scratch, and was given the rank of first officer. In her smart navy-blue uniform with its gold-embroidered wings, Diana was eventually posted to No 15 Ferry Pilot Pool at Hamble in Hampshire. Of all the ATA airfields, Hamble was very much in the front line, and yet its complement of pilots was exclusively female.

Sandwiched between the Southampton Water and the River Hamble, it had the balloon barrages of Portsmouth and Gosport on one side and those of Eastleigh and Southampton on the other—posing considerable hazards to all pilots in the region. It was not just light air-

above and right: Air Transport Auxiliary
pilot Diana Barnato-Walker

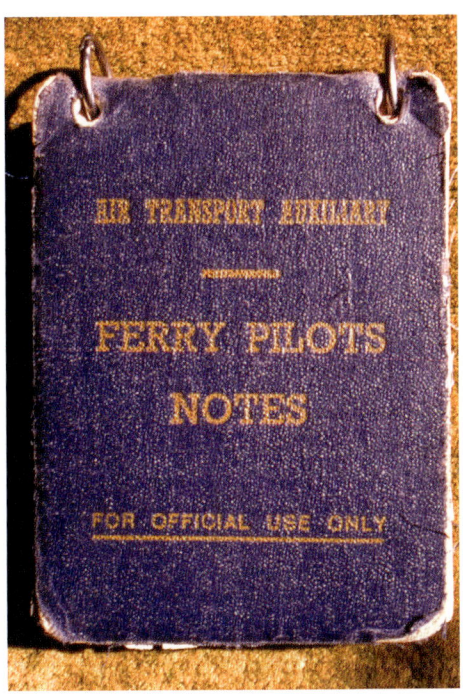

craft such as Tiger Moths which these Hamble girls flew. Their proximity to the Hamble Spitfire building and repair facility and the Eastleigh Spitfire factory meant that the girls handled primarily fighter aircraft. But they were also required to deliver Hudsons, Mitchells, Blenheims, and Oxfords, as well as Walrus and Sea Otter amphibians and many other types. The girls had to be adaptable. One moment they could be expected to fly a Blackburn Roc, then a Proctor and then a Mitchell. During the 1944 invasion period they were delivering upward of twenty fighters a day—Typhoons, Tempests, Mustangs, and Spitfires—directly to the forward airfields on the south coast, from where RAF squadrons flew them straight into action over France.

Diana recalled a typical day at Hamble: "We would be waiting around for the weather to clear—writing letters, playing bridge, listening to the wireless, sewing. Suddenly, the loudspeaker would blare out 'All pilots report to the Operations Room for their chits.' Everyone would immediately drop whatever she happened to be doing and go to the hatchway to be briefed for her job for the day. There would be a mad scurry into the lockers for maps and helmet, a visit to Met for the weather information, then off to the Maps and Signals office for the latest news about stray balloons and airfield serviceability. If a pilot got a type of aircraft she had not flown before it would be off to the library for a book of 'handling notes' which would tell her all she needed to know about flying that type."

The girls trudged out to the taxi aircraft, hugging parachutes and overnight bags, and one of their number would have been assigned the duty of taxi pilot, ferrying the girls by Anson to their starting points and collecting them all again

The Women
Airforce Service
Pilots

at the end of the day.

Home for Diana was a rented cottage shared with one of the other girls. "We all got on well together, we had to. There was no bitchiness and we worked together well as a team under the guidance of Commander Margot Gore." This team of women at 15 FPP was a multinational one with girls from Denmark, Poland, Argentina, South Africa, Chile, Australia, and the United States alongside the British contingent.

It was the American girls who formed the largest foreign group. Jacqueline Cochran, a New York businesswoman, had begun to recruit likely women candidates for the ATA. Among them was a twenty-year-old office clerk, Emily Chapin. With just a minimum of flying hours, she bravely traveled to England by cargo boat

across the U-boat-patrolled Atlantic and joined the ATA in August 1942. Soon she qualified as pilot with the rank of third officer and was attached to the Hamble-based No 15 Pool.

Apart from the hazards of the English weather, balloon barrages, inexperience on so many aircraft types and unfamiliar terrain, there was also the unexpected. Emily was only just airborne in a Spitfire when a defective latch caused the hood to blow open. Unable to close it, she came in for an emergency landing, but with her wind-blurred vision she misjudged the approach. The Spitfire dropped on one wheel and the wing scraped along the concrete; it then bounced hard onto its other wheel, severely damaging the other wing. By the end of the runway the airplane was a wreck and Emily was badly shaken but unhurt. Shortly after this incident, the unpredictable weather claimed Emily's American friend Mary Nicholson, who flew into a mist-shrouded hillside and was killed instantly.

When Jacqueline Cochran later contacted Emily about a new organization being set up in the States for women pilots, she decided to go home and join the Women Airforce Service Pilots—WASPs for short. Reluctantly the ATA released her. Emily Chapin and her compatriots gave selfless and invaluable service to Britain in her hour of need.

During the Second World War, 174 ATA pilots were killed—men and women. Tanya Whittall, Dora Lang, Honor Salmon, and Pat Walker, all from 15 FPP, Hamble, were among those who died, as well as Mary Nicholson. Amy Johnson was also among the ATA casualties. If combat fighter pilots were heroes, these girls were surely heroines. They were certainly exceptional women doing vital work. The ATA, however, was not an exclusively female organization. Its male pilots were generally men with flying experience who, if over twenty-five, were considered too old for operational RAF service. Many were World War I fliers, some were prewar airline captains, club pilots, or barnstormers. Some were disabled, but all were united in purpose and in their love of flying. It was sometimes joked that ATA really stood for "Ancient and Tattered Airmen."

When war broke out, Len Biggs was one of those too old to join the RAF for flying duties. The Air Ministry didn't even bother to reply to his applications. He was discouraged, but knew that as a healthy thirty-five-year-old he had something worthwhile to offer his country. One day he happened to hear on the radio that pilots under fifty, with a minimum of fifty hours' flying experience, were required for work of national importance. As an ex-club pilot, he qualified and immediately applied and was told to go home and await instructions. Six weeks later he was at White Waltham and in ATA uniform as First Officer Biggs.

Len was posted to Whitchurch, near Bristol, where his unit was delivering Beaufighters to and from the Bristol aircraft works. He remembered: "The Beaufighter was not the easiest of airplanes to fly, but it was exciting. Many pilots were scared to death of them, but if in difficulties I'd rather be in a Beau than anything else. When you put her through the gate there was this massive surge of sheer power and you'd leap into the air. It had immense strength too. One of our pilots, 'Timber' Woods, hated Beaus and one day spread one all over Sealand aerodrome. He made the most frightful landing you can imagine—the tail section broke

Women Airforce Service Pilots on the wing of a P-47 Thunderbolt fighter.

off, the engine shot out and he was left sitting in what remained of the center section. If it had been anything other than a Beaufighter he'd have been dead."

Sometimes the ferry pilots would show the fighter boys how things were done. "On one occasion we had a pilot on our Pool deliver an urgently needed Spitfire to a fighter squadron. The weather was dreadful. So bad, in fact, that the fighter pilots were all grounded. Who could this be, they asked, flying on a day when they, the real 'ace' pilots, were all grounded? Well, this particular pilot was an elderly gentleman with a gray beard and, to give them something to think about, he produced a walking stick, struggled arthritically from the cockpit, and limped away before an astonished audience."

Humor, of course, played an important role in maintaining morale. "On the Hurricane, the radiator was slung in the center, so that when on the ground the propwash kept it cool. On the Spit though, it was offset so that you had to be careful when taxiing or running the engine up on the ground, that you didn't overheat. One day I was taxiing a Spit round the perimeter track when I came across a truck parked in my way. It was impossible to go round it off the track because it was winter and the ground was very soft, so I revved the engine to attract attention. After ages they moved, but by then the temperature had shot up and up so that when I finally parked I was furious. I complained to the ground crew and said that I was boiling and my temperature had shot up to a hundred and twenty degrees. Later, I was in the watch office complaining about the truck when two medical orderlies dashed in excitedly carrying a stretcher and breathlessly inquired, 'Where's the

pilot with the high temperature?'"

Like Len, Diana Barnato flew most fighter and twin-engined types during her time with the ATA, but regretted not getting her hands on all of them. "The RAF only had a few of some aircraft and the rarer ones which came through the ATA were all flown by those we called 'type catchers.'" Everything else, though, seemed to appear in her logbook and before she

reached her twenty-second birthday she had flown no fewer than 260 Spitfires. They were mainly delivery flights of brand new airplanes, or transiting flights of Spitfires to be modified, or the return of repaired aircraft for squadron use. To Diana and the other girls of 15 FPP, such flights were routine. But there was one very special delivery.

During 1944, Diana had married

Wing Commander Derek Walker, a Typhoon pilot who had been appointed assistant to Air Vice Marshal Coningham, the air officer commanding, RAF 2nd Tactical Air Force. When Derek phoned one day to say that he had a Spitfire that urgently needed delivering to Belgium, the opportunity of spending some time together on leave in newly liberated Brussels seemed too good to miss.

Diana recalled: "Although France and the Low Countries had been liberated, the offical policy was that these places were still out of bounds to ATA women. It was said that there were still pockets of German resistance, and that facilities were basic and primitive and not fit for females. The girls at Hamble were upset to say the least. We really wanted to get over there and, with Hamble so

close, it was doubly frustrating. When Derek phoned to ask if I would fly the Spitfire PR VII, a photo-reconnaissance Mark VII, to Evers, near Brussels, I was thrilled, but said I could only do it if he got special permission. In due course he produced a letter signed by AVM Coningham and I booked some days leave. Meeting Derek at Northolt near London, I took MD174 and flew in formation with him down to Tangmere, Derek in his personal Spitfire. Outbound from Tangmere, we crossed over the Channel and when we reached the French coast I could see a stretch of sandy beach which was completely covered by bomb craters. It was an awesome sight. The experience of this flight, in formation with my husband, was exhilarating and we subsequently spent a wonderful few days in Brussels. On the day we were to leave, the airfield was fogbound. There was no hope of getting back, so I got permission to extend my leave for a couple of days. Even then, on the day I was due out, the weather was still poor, but Derek said it might not be so bad once we were airborne. So we took off and I formated on Derek and stuck close to him in thick cloud, fog and haze. My Spitfire was to be returned to England, complete with rolls of exposed film still in the cameras, the airplane having been flown over enemy lines and the pictures needed back in London. Derek told me not to put down in France if I had a problem, but to head back for England if I could. I had a little bit of difficulty staying with Derek anyway, because the RAF flew at higher revs and boost than ATA pilots and, in any case, we always flew alone, never in formation. When I looked away from Derek's Spitfire for one second, he was gone. He'd vanished into cloud and I was on my own. Looking

top right: Modern counterparts, female F-15 Eagle fighter pilots of the U.S. Air Force.

around, I saw a plane in the distance and, thinking it was Derek, flew off to see. It was a Dakota going the other way. So I had to sort things out for myself. I had no radio and even if I had, I wouldn't have been able to use it because we never flew with radio in the ATA. I went down low to have a look and try to see where I was. Down on the deck I ran into some thick clag of cloud and I knew I had to climb to get over the hills around St. Omer. I reached the coast eventually and, in looking down, I could see what I was sure was that same pock-marked sandbar I'd seen on the way in. Confidently setting 317 degrees, I calculated that Dungeness would be my landfall in seven and a half minutes. There was sea fog just above the deck so I went over it and after seven and a half minutes I glanced down to see that there was still water between the gaps in the low yellow fog. It was a heart-stopping moment. Where was I? What had gone wrong? I concluded that my point of departure from the Continent must have

been much farther north than I had imagined and that 317 degrees could be taking me up the North Sea where I would soon vanish when the petrol ran out. But if I had left the French coast farther south, then I was possibly flying up the middle of the English Channel. So I turned west for a few minutes more, and then on to due north so that I would be able to get to the south coast of England. I flew just above the sea avoid the yellow fog and thought I would climb above it when I knew I must be over land and then bail out. Contemplating the awfulness of my predicament, I suddenly saw a white gleam dead ahead. The white cliffs of Dover? No, it wasn't Dover. Where was this? Bognor Regis. Yes, that was the Bognor gasometer. I didn't suppose anyone before or since has been so glad to see the Bognor gas-works, but at least I now knew where I was. Tangmere was just a few miles inland and the fog was so thick that I flew up river to Chichester, round the cathedral and into Tangmere. As

I taxied up to the watch office I could see a Spitfire parked outside. It was Derek's. White-faced, he asked me what had happened. All of England was fogged in. He had been told on his radio that Tangmere was the only aerodrome open. How had I found it? 'Oh, no problem,' I told him."

Not all of Diana's flights were so dramatic, but there were other worrying moments. On one occasion, a large fuselage portion of the Typhoon she was ferrying fell off in the air, leaving nothing beneath her feet. She managed to land the unstable airplane, but it was still a write-off. The watch office clerk, known to the girls as "Ned in the shed," scolded her as she taxied the crippled Typhoon in. "Whatever are you doing, Miss Barnato, bringing me only half an airplane."

Flying a new type, or a modified mark of an otherwise familiar plane, could be disconcerting. A Ford-based RAF Mosquito squadron had taken heavy losses and now, to add to their unease, were about to be re-equipped

above: Former WASPs attending a reunion; below: A WASP in an AT-6 trainer at Avenger Field during the war.

with a new type of Mosquito. It was Margot Gore's girls at Hamble who were to deliver the new kites and Margot had a confidence-boosting trick up her sleeve for the RAF pilots. "We were all told to look our best—smart uniforms, lipstick, make-up and our hair done so that when the boys saw all these pretty young things climbing out of their new mark Mossies, they'd know that they could certainly fly them. But there was a master stroke to Margot's plan. One of our number, Lois Butler, was a grandmother, although still in her thirties. Lois arrived last and we girls stood around chatting to the RAF pilots, craning our necks and straining our eyes for the straggler. 'Where's Grandma?' we asked. Grandma? The reaction was as planned. A grandma flying Mosquitos? Soon, Lois arrived, landed, climbed out, and took off her flying helmet, shaking her hair out as she did so. The effect was perfect. If young girls and grandmothers could fly these new beasts anyone could."

By the end of hostilities and the standdown of ATA, its pilots had completed a staggering 309,011 aircraft movements and collected CBEs, OBEs, MBEs, George Medals, and other decorations in recognition of invaluable and heroic service. The unofficial and fitting motto of the Air Transport Auxiliary was Aetheris Avidia, "Eager for the Air."

They were called WASPs, the Women Airforce Service Pilots, an organization of pioneering civilian American female aviators established to fly military aircraft in ferrying, target towing, and other roles during the Second World War, thus freeing thousands of male pilots for combat service and related duties. WASP was a volunteer organization formed in September 1942 when U.S. Army

Air Force recruiters and newspapers called for young women to apply. Some 25,000 answered the call and of these, 1,830 were accepted for training; 1,074 completed the flight training, having re-learned to fly "the Army way." On graduating, each WASP was awarded her wings.

Initially, the WASP had come from two predecessor groups called the WAFS, the Women's Auxiliary Ferrying Squadron, and the WFTD, the Women's Flying Training Detachment. The women of the WAFS were all well-qualified pilots and had been assigned directly as civilian ferry pilots with the Second Ferrying Group at New Castle Army Air Base, Wilmington, Delaware, where they were checked out on military aircraft. Their leader was twenty-eight-year-old Nancy Love, a highly experienced pilot who had a thorough knowledge of the Ferrying Division of the Air Transport Command. Her husband, Major Robert M. Love, was administrative executive of the Ferrying Command.

The well-known aviator and racing pilot, Jacqueline Cochran, was director of the Women's Flying Training Detachment in Houston, Texas, and her graduates were then assigned to the Air Transport Command as ferry pilots delivering various Army Air Force aircraft from the factories to and from the air bases. Cochran's school began a new class of trainees each month from November 1942 through April 1944 with the last class graduating in December 1944.

The WAFS and the WFTD were ultimately merged in August 1943 to form the WASP. With the merger, Miss Cochran was appointed director of women pilots; Mrs. Love was made WASP executive with the staff of the Ferrying Division, Air Transport Command.

The derelict art deco former headquarters of the ATA at White Waltham airfield near London.

General Henry H. "Hap" Arnold, commanding general of the Army Air Forces, had planned for the WASP, a civil service program, to eventually be militarized, but that was not to be. On June 21, 1944, the U.S. House of Representatives of the Congress narrowly defeated a House bill to give the WASP military status. Civilian male pilots had lobbied against the bill in reaction to the closing of several civilian flight training schools and termination of two male pilot training commissioning programs. A House Committee on the Civil Service had reported on June 5 that, in its opinion, the WASP was unnecessary and unjustifably expensive, recommending a halt in the recruitment and training of new WASPs. By June, many in the Congress believed that the war was coming to an end with it the need for the WASP. The Army Air Force had by then developed an excess of both trained pilots and pilot candidates and, as a result, General Arnold ordered the disbanding of the WASP by December 20, 1944.

". . . WASPs from all over the country were heading for Sweetwater, Texas. Marge Gilbert, Carol White, and I arrived in Sweetwater, tired and dirty. The ride across Texas had jostled us unmercifully, and the open windows had assailed us with wind, dust, and the odors of Texas sage, gas, and oil. Having lived in the East and the Midwest, I had never before seen anything like this wide, empty landscape, these miles and miles of open range. Surprised and fascinated, I could not keep my eyes away from this unusual and captivating scene.

"At the station, 'cattle wagons' from Avenger Field greeted us. The 'cattle wagon' was a large, primitive sort of bus. All windows and hard seats, this 'people-mover' transport-

ed WASPs to auxiliary fields or to any other place they needed to go. We loaded our belongings into its spacious interior and hung on as the monster lurched into gear and rattled its way along the highway to our base, Avenger Field.

" 'Avenger Field,' a magic name for all us hopefuls, certainly lived up to our expectations. The roar of the planes, the low, wooden barracks so close to the flight line, the mess hall, the huge marching field—and the sand—everywhere, the sand. As Lorraine Zillner says, 'It was so wonderful. We all were bright-eyed, excited; it was all so new to us. The routine, the militarization, the way we had to march to classes, and the hours we had to keep—most of us weren't used to that.

"One of the first things the officers did (which will be familiar to anyone who was ever in the Air Force) was to line us up and tell us to look at the person on either side of us. We were then told that both of those people would wash out. Of course, someone would be looking at you from each side. We were supposed to be impressed that this was a very difficult program. More than half did wash out, but Sadie Hawkins was not at all impressed. 'Remember,' she says, 'when they told us to look on either side of you, because probably both of them would wash out? I just thought "Poor things." It never occurred to me that I would wash out.' "
—from *Women Pilots of World War II* by Jean Hascall Cole

"Soon they were taking off, three at a time, with their instructors, in the little open-cockpit trainers. As more classes arrived at Avenger Field, there would be as many as fifty planes in the air at one time. As the tower had not yet been completed to regulate air traffic,

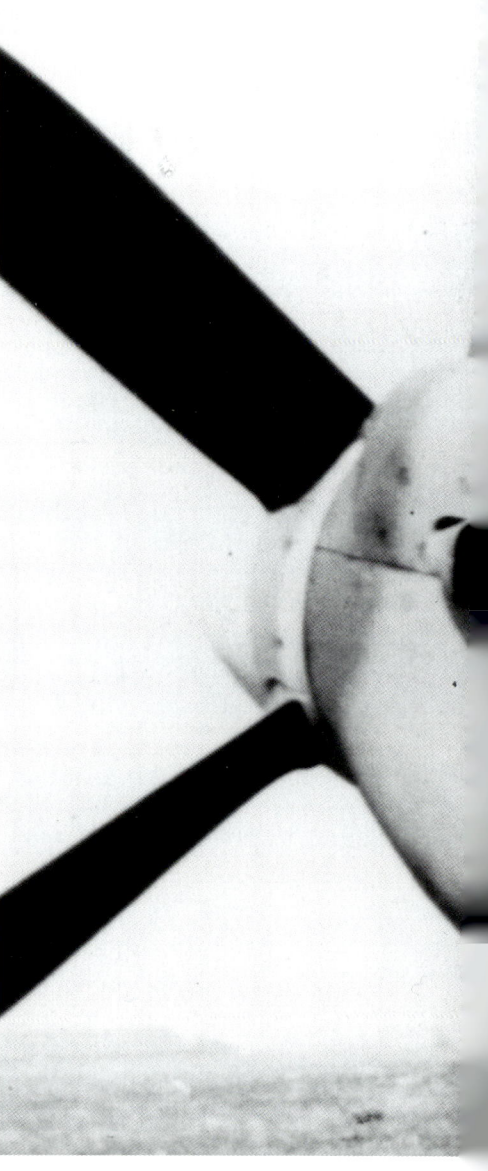

A wartime image of ATA pilots on a late mark Spitfire.

ATA First Officer Maureen Dunlop.

43-5 trainees developed the eyes of hawks in a matter of days. In the traffic pattern, they flew stacked four or five levels high as they circled and dropped down to the next level until it was their turn to land.

"From the air, they saw that west Texas was perfectly laid out for flying. All the roads were navigational aids—they ran north-south and east-west. As trainees approached the Avenger Field runway, however, their troubles began. One of the runways was almost always under construction, so from their first day of training every landing was cross-wind, or perpendicular to the wind. They had to learn to dodge tiny cyclones filled with dust, called dust devils, which danced around the runways and could tip up a wing in a second. Also hazardous on landing were meandering flocks of tumbleweed which could jump up at an airplane to become entangled in the landing gear, or entwined in the propeller. The trainees did not know it, but they were getting the best of flight training, mainly because of the habitat.

"One day a trainee could not resist taking a sunbath. She soon learned that, though Cochran's Convent was off limits to male cadets, in the skies trainees were fair game. She trimmed the PT perfectly so that it flew itself, held by the stick between her knees. Checking for other aircraft in the area and seeing none, she took her shirt off and leaned back, her face pointed toward the sun. After several luxurious minutes, she heard an unexpected roar. Opening her eyes, she saw two other PTs on either side of her. Soon she was surrounded by a flock of primary trainers. In the cockpits were not women trainees from Avenger Field, but male cadets who were grinning and waving enthusiastically. Her PT began to weave and bob as she fumbled with her shirt in the windy

cockpit. Then the shirt slipped out of her hands and sailed out over the Texas plains. Above the roar of the engines, her aerial audience cheered. She ducked down in the cockpit, and sneaking looks over the side, banked steeply and headed back toward Avenger Field. When she landed, she taxied to the flight line, cut the engine and from a seemingly empty cockpit, waiting trainees heard a voice yell, 'Somebody bring me a blanket.'"
—from *Those Wonderful Women in Their Flying Machines* by Sally VanWagenen Keil

Meanwhile. . . "250 miles north of Sweetwater in Canyon, Texas, Lela Loudder's mother finally signed a waiver allowing her daughter to join the Women Airforce Service Pilots. Lela's parents had been staunch in their refusal throughout three days of tears, until her older sister came up with the winning argument. 'After all, Lela has been on her own for months,' her sister reasoned, 'down in Corpus Christi—with the navy!'

"That afternoon Lela ran into Nell Stevenson, who had been in Civilian Pilot Training with her during college. Lela could barely wait to tell her what she was up to, but Nell beat her to it. Two hometown girls going into the Army Air Force flight training was big news in Canyon, and the postmaster said that he had even been questioned about both of them by an FBI agent. A security check! That was something, Lela thought. She knew she was going to be involved in important work!

"In the middle of June Lela and Nell wheedled a tank of gas at the Chevrolet dealership and drove from Canyon to Avenger Field. They stopped on the outskirts of Sweetwater to ask directions to the airfield. About three miles the other

side of town, they were told, and then up a gravel road another mile or so. Before they reached the turnoff, they could see the planes and hear the engines roar.

"Lela and Nell slipped into the air base's administrative offices to join the flock of frightened girls, disguised like themselves in hats, gloves, and high heels, warily eyeing one another and waiting for something to happen. Some had their sophisticated finery rumpled by long journeys across the prairie, while others looked fresher than they felt after spending a tense, sleepless night at the Blue Bonnet Hotel in town—but they were all doing their best to seem nonchalant and knowing. Lela thought a cigarette would have helped, but a sign read NO SMOKING.

"Before long a stern Army Air Force officer in starched khakis greeted the new class with a list of rules and warnings, and handed out printed copies. Then a small, dark-haired woman, who spoke with homey authority and introduced herself as Mrs. Deaton, assured the rookies that their families would be notified they had reached Sweetwater safe and sound. Eyeing the mound of suitcases and trunks surrounding the girls, she added, 'Since there is only one footlocker per girl in each bay, you will be allowed to store surplus baggage here in the office—until arrangements are made to ship it home.'

"This caused a scramble. What ought to stay? Yes, one night a week they'd need a dress for dinner.

"What could they do without? 'Large musical instruments and golf clubs might not be appropriate— under the circumstances.'

"Deaton told them to form groups of six, pick up their bed linens at the laundry, and find a bay in the barracks. The one hundred girls in Lela's class

devoted the next couple of hours to getting acquainted with each other— and their new living quarters.

"Two showers—two mirrors— for twelve of us? They've got to be kidding! Sweetie, would you mind switching cots with me? . . . hey, well, you can't shoot a gal for trying! My God, I didn't know this was what she meant by a footlocker. She's got to be kidding! A friend in 43-4 told me a girl got killed last week with her instructor—night flying. No, I am not kidding. The plane burned! They didn't find the bodies until the next morning. The plane burned? Her name was Jane Champlin. She was in my friend's class."
—from *On Silver Wings* by Marianne Verges

The taxi Anson's piled with flying kit, each ferry pilot cons his morning chit, when from the weather office comes the cry that to the west black clouds bestride the sky. Then out "Met's" head is thrust from windows wide this dark portent to ponder or deride; 'tis dull, 'tis dark, the cloud's precipitating, no weather this for us to aviate in! But one more bold by far than all the rest out to the runway taxis, gazes west, raises an eyebrow, casts his eyes about, wriggles his corns, his shoulder blades, his snout. Instinct at work— will it be wet or fine? What does this Flying Weather seer divine? He turns about and trundles back to "Met" to tell them that it really will be wet.
—anonymous ATA pilot

FOREIGN FIGHTERS

Pilots of many nations fought with the RAF and the Americans against the German Air Force in the Second World War. The pilot of this Spitfire comes from New Zealand.

Such indomitable courage and determination cannot go unrewarded, and when this war is won we must see that Poland is again restored to her former liberty and freedom, which her sons fought so valiantly to maintain.
—Flight Lieutenant D. M. Crook

"THEY KNEW WHY THEY WERE HERE," remarked a senior RAF officer of foreign fighter pilots in the World War II Royal Air Force. His comment was a tribute to the exceptional determination of those non-British airmen who formed an important element of Fighter Command. Airmen from at least thirteen nations took part in the Battle of Britain and this tally increased as the war progressed. Czechs, Poles, Belgians, Dutch, Free French, Norwegians, and at least one Icelander took part, in addition to other English-speaking nationalities including Canadians, Americans, South Africans, Australians, and New Zealanders. But it was mainly the non-English speaking nationals of whom it was said that "they knew why they were here." Almost without exception they had escaped Nazi occupation, had left behind families and loved ones, had endured dreadful hardships in their efforts to reach England . . . and none knew if or when they would be going home. Half a century later Kazimierz Budzik still had the keen eyes and quick reflexes of a fighter pilot. It was easy to imagine him in the role.

Commissioned as a second lieutenant in the Polish Air Force the day war broke out, Budzik had a depressingly short career as a fighter pilot in his native country before fleeing the Nazis to continue the fight from France. There he flew Potez and Dewoitine fighters from Pol air base near the Pyrenees until France fell. The French helped to get him and other Poles to Casablanca via ferry

and then to Gibraltar, from where he was finally able to sail for England by convoy.

At Liverpool, Budzik was sent for training and posted to No 308 (Polish) Squadron, flying Spitfires. He joined an air force that was just going on the offensive, a course perfectly suited to his temperament. Born in Lekawica, a district of Kraków, it was appropriate that Budzik should have been posted to 308, the City of Kraków Squadron. It was based at Northolt near London and was primarily engaged in bomber-escort missions and offensive sweeps over France.

Modest to a fault, Budzik dismisses any suggestion of heroism. "Heroes? I don't know what they are. There were brave deeds done, of course. Mostly, though, heroes were born out of spur-of-the-moment actions. Most of the time I was concerned with self-preservation, like everyone else." But his logbook tells its own story. Two operational tours of duty . . . tally upon tally of ops flown . . . dogfights . . . night-fighter patrols . . . strafing attacks . . . dive-bombing missions . . . bomber-escort missions . . . being shot down twice . . . and a score of kills or probables to which this exceptional man reluctantly admits. As he jabs a finger at an entry in his log, the memory of a particular combat prompts comment: "Probably I should have claimed that one. I know I hit him . . . yes . . . that 190 was mine. I know it." Even his commanding officer urged him to claim it, but Kaz wouldn't bother. What did it matter? That he'd got it was important to him. He didn't need to advertise the fact. Tomorrow there might be another. Perhaps he'd count that one. Reflecting on that particular combat, he commented on the tendency of the Polish pilots to become impatient and overexcitable in air combat. "We always, always opened fire much too early. The English seemed to have more patience and self-control, waiting until they had got in close or maneuvered into the best position before opening fire." That tendency may have cost Budzik and his fellow Poles a considerable number of victories. With precious few seconds of ammunition, the available rounds were soon gone in a careless, out-of-range hosing of the sky.

As an exclusively Polish squadron, 308 used their native tongue during RT conversation in the air. "Most of us knew little English, and in any case, if in a tight corner or shouting a warning of danger, we'd be fumbling around for the right English words and someone would have soon been dead." Quick reactions were, of course, fundamental to fighter piloting. As Kaz put it, "You had to do it before you had thought about it." But one young Pole posted to Budzik's squadron, Pilot Officer Jan Wiejski, just didn't have those lightning reactions. Budzik, by now an old hand, saw that the new boy was not up to it. "'Now look here,' I told him. 'Why not see the CO about a transfer to another squadron? You just won't make it otherwise. Bombers, or Coastal Command, perhaps, is your thing.'" Wiejski knew that Budzik was right. But he'd not change now. He'd see it through. Sadly, Budzik's judgement proved correct.

"We were escorting bombers, but the operation just didn't go properly to plan. On the way back we saw a group of FW 190s. I was one of the last in my section of six aircraft and, watching the 190s, we didn't see another group of them coming from behind. Suddenly, something in my mirror. A flash. Instinctively, I swerved and pulled around tightly toward our attackers and was head-on to about

ten . . . maybe twenty . . . 190s. The next few seconds were spent just trying to survive. I did, but the rest of my flight, five aircraft in all, were shot down. Among them was Jan Wiejski. It was his first operational trip. He didn't stand a chance."

As the war continued, the German fighter opposition over France, Belgium, and Holland seemed to diminish. When there was a dogfight, it would be over in seconds. In and out. Attacking or evading. That was the battle. Often the two opposing formations would climb and circle miles from each other, vying for the advan-tage of height or sun. Then it would suddenly be over. The German forma-tion would dive away without a shot being fired. It was frustrating for the boys of 308 to return to base without having pressed the gun button.

Once the Normandy invasion got under way, however, that frustration ended. As an element of the 2nd Tactical Air Force, Budzik's squadron was deployed in the ground attack / close support role. Flying Spitfire XIVs equipped with cannon and bombs, there was a lot of satisfaction in knowing that they were deliver-ing real damage to the enemy. "I

Kazimierz Budzik flew briefly with the Polish air force before fleeing the Nazis to fly with the French. He then made his way to England where, after additional training, he was posted to No 308 (Polish) Squadron at RAF Northolt in the north of London. Surviving the war, Kaz was awarded the Polish VC (the Virtuti Militari), the Polish Cross of Valor four times and the Polish Air Force Medal four times.

flew what must have been dozens of flights during the struggle for the Falaise Pocket. I don't mind admitting to a feeling of glee and excitement because, on the ground, I could see Jerries by the score looking up at me . . . terrified. Some of them had their hands above their heads as I roared over them. I remember thinking, Now you bastards, how do you like it? It was a different story in 1939, though. They showed Poland no mercy then, but here they were now, begging for it. It was a wonderful experience."

About this time Budzik's squadron aircraft were being fitted with a new gyro gunsight. This remarkable innovation greatly increased the accuracy of shooting and made automatic corrections for deflection, largely eliminating human error—but not Polish impatience and excitement. Budzik was to discover this to his cost. "They fitted these sights, but they never trained us how to use them. Instead, we had to find out for ourselves. Well, for air-to-ground work . . . no problem. You just put the dot on the target and simply hit it. You couldn't miss. Of course, by this time, intervention by German fighters was comparatively rare. We just got on with our lovely job of bombing and shooting things up on the ground. Then, one day, there was a shout of 'Focke Wulf' over the radio. 'I'll get him!' I called, diving after him absolutely flat out. He was in my sights . . . rrrrrrrmmp . . . nothing. Not a single hit. Problem was that these wonderful new gyro sights needed a second or two to settle. I hadn't allowed for that. My impatience and excitemenrt wouldn't let me. But now the chase was on. Down on the deck we were streaking for Germany.

I wouldn't let him get there. No. Was that smoke or exhaust fumes I could see trailing out behind? Well, it soon would be smoke. In my sights . . . gyro settled now . . . fire! Nothing. All my ammo had gone in that first burst that had missed. But at least I had learned about gyro gunsights."

But it was the ground-attack role that proved to be the most dangerous for Budzik. "After the invasion, we had been flying from Ghent in Belgium and were tasked to carry out a dive-bombing attack on Walcheren Island off the Dutch

left: A Polish squadron Spitfire escorting a B-17 of the 92nd Bomb Group; below: A Polish Sergeant Pilot, Nick Kosiuk, with his Wellington bomber.

Canadian Johnny Kent, second from left, led No 303 (Polish) Squadron at RAF Northolt throughout the Battle of Britain.

coast. As we approached the target a terrific amount of flak came up from all directions. When that happened, we learned that we could tease the gunners by holding off just out of range of their guns; then we'd judge the moment to dive when the fire had slackened off, or maybe we'd fool the gunners into thinking that we were going away, Often this ploy worked quite well. But on this occasion I remember I was trembling with fear. Everyone experiences fear, but for me the fear went once we had committed ourselves to the attack—although the trembling soon returned. I was leading my section in when suddenly *wham* I quickly turned the aircraft around and, despite the damage, I managed to get it down in a crash-landing. Once I was down, everything seemed so quiet, and yet, as I got out of the cockpit there was the sound of a ground battle all around me—heavy gunfire, rifles and machine guns. I quickly got myself to a ditch and thought that this was not a good situation for a fighter pilot to be in. Then some civilians turned up. From a distance I shouted to them, 'Go away!' and waved my pistol around to reinforce my request. I was worried that they might turn me over to the Germans. But then a woman among them shouted in English, 'Are you British?' 'No, Polish.' Where are the British? I answered back. Back came the reply, 'Down the road. We're waiting for them.' Once identities and allegiances had been established the civilians came closer and a man with a bicycle approached and said he'd take me to the British lines. I hopped on the bike and went off with him, but before I did, I produced my pistol again and told him I'd shoot him if he was taking me to the Germans. He didn't, so I didn't have to shoot

Little Friends, the escort fighters, accompanying B-17s of the 390th Bomb Group on a mission to a German target in 1943; right: Squadron Leader A. G. Lewis of Kimberly, South Africa, was credited with eighteen aerial victories in his service with the RAF.

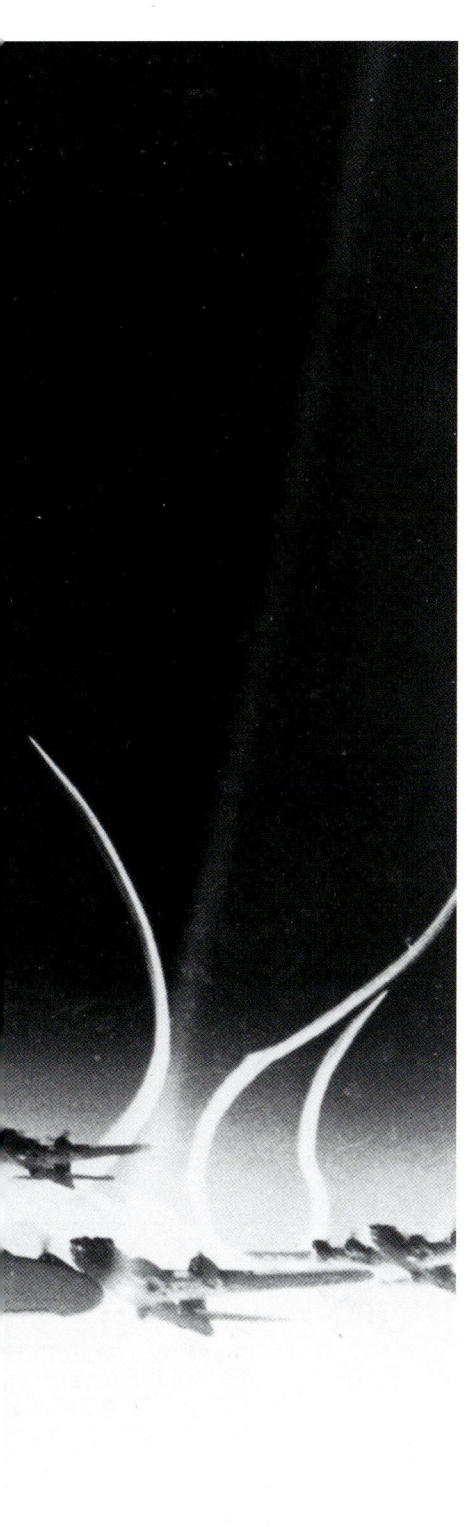

ORDE
29 Dec 1940

South African fighter ace and superb
air leader, Adolph "Sailor" Malan, in a
wartime drawing by Cuthbert Orde.

him after all, and gave him cigarettes instead of lead."

Almost immediately, Budzik was back flying ops and very soon was shot down again. Once more it was ground fire and once more he survived. His luck held. He had survived through two tours of duty, but after two crash-landings he was sure he wouldn't be lucky a third time, though he kept his fears to himself. So many friends had gone and his turn was surely coming. "By this stage of the war I was really nervous about flak. Quite jumpy. But then I had reason to be. Twice it had nearly killed me. Even so, to a certain extent we fighters could get out of the way of flak—not like the bombers. Once, while escorting Mitchells over Le Havre, the flak was too intense for us so we simply moved off away from the bombers, which were attracting the gunfire. Suddenly one of the B-25s in the center of the formation took a direct hit and went down, but the formation just plowed right on. The most amazing thing was to see another bomber slide into the position from where the other aircraft had just been lost. To me, that took guts."

The war was coming to an end; Budzik would survive, and Helen, a pretty young Polish WAAF, had agreed to marry him, though they shared the sadness of being unable to return home to a free Poland. He was awarded the Polish VC (the Virtuti Militari), the Polish Cross of Valor four times and the Polish Air Force Medal four times. His portrait by Slawa Sadlowska appeared in her 1947 *Album of Polish Airmen* side by side with the fellow pilots he revered.

Kaz Budzik was lucky. It was not just his skill that kept a fighter pilot alive in World War II. Luck played a major part. Shooting prowess and airmanship counted for nothing when catastrophic aircraft failure occurred, and a great number of pilots were killed in such accidents rather than in combat. One such was Flight Sergeant Emil Samuelsen of the Royal Norwegian Air Force.

Samuelsen was considered to be one of Norway's most capable military pilots. Born in Tjolling in 1918, he grew up in a large family and seemed set for a career at sea when the war changed the course of his life and Norway fell to the Germans in 1940. He was serving as assistant engineer on a whaling factory ship, the SS *Kosmos II*, and instead of returning home to occupied Norway the *Kosmos* sailed for England, where Emil discharged himself from the ship's company and enlisted in the Norwegian army. Army life did not suit him, though, and by August of that year, inspired by the exploits of "The Few," he transferred to the Royal Norwegian Air Force for pilot training.

He was sent to Canada to the "Little Norway" training facilities for Norwegian airmen at Toronto and Moose Jaw. There he earned his wings. Along the way, though, there was the drama of an emergency landing with wheels retracted on a Dakota. Unhurt, Samuelsen was commended for his skill in saving the aircraft.

From Canada, Emil followed the well-trodden route to an operational unit via an operational training unit: 58 OTU at Grangemouth. On August 19, 1942, he was posted to North Weald in Essex to No 332 (Norwegian) Squadron, flying Spitfire Vs, where he performed well and showed great promise.

On January 27, 1943, flying one of 332's new Mark IX Spitfires, Samuelsen was doing routine air test. He was seen to perform a 250 mph aileron-reflex check over North Weald and to fly straight and level across the field shortly after. Then, climbing to complete a 400 mph test, he was lost to view as the Spitfire entered cloud. Moments later it reappeared in a high-speed vertical dive, clearly out of control.

At Brick House Farm, near Matching Green, the occupants heard the roar of the stricken plane directly overhead. The impact, when it came, was devastating. Plaster came down from the ceilings, windows cracked, and pictures fell from walls. Then silence.

Emil's Spitfire had missed the house by yards, but sliced instead through the roof of a nearby barn. When rescuers approached the smoking hole, it was apparent that there was no hope for the pilot. The impact had driven the Spitfire deep beneath the earthen floor of the barn, taking Emil Samuelsen with it. It was a tragic end for a man described by Hans Jörgensen, his boyhood friend, as "among the cream of the cream of Norway's youth."

At Honor Oak Crematorium, London, nearly the entire complement of 332 Squadron turned out for Emil's funeral; the coffin decorated with the Norwegian flag and a wreath from King Haakon VII. After the war his ashes were returned to Larvik on the shores of Oslo Fjord and close by his birthplace. Unlike Kaz Budzik, he had gone home.

The story of Emil Samuelsen has a postscript. In 1989, the cement screed floor of the repaired barn at Brick House Farm cracked and caved in. As it was dug out for repair, pieces of metal shining in the bottom of the hole—a wheel, cannon shells, and bits of wing—were revealed. Poignant reminders of one life lost among the many who were Britain's "foreign fighter friends."

GERMAN ESCORT

IN 1940–41 SOME FORTUNATE LUFTWAFFE fighter pilots on the Channel coast of France were living well in the comfort of requisitioned chateaux. Most, though, were living in the field under canvas. But, early in the war, they were buoyed by easy victories and confident that the impending fight with the Royal Air Force would be yet another quick skirmish with conclusive results. That illusion was quickly shattered. There would be no walkover and the German pilot would have a lot to worry about.

The British pilot was fighting for the survival of his homeland. He had the psychological advantage—and powerful incentive—of flying and fighting above his own country. For the German there was the daunting prospect of overflying the sea to England, followed by combat over alien territory and then another flight back across water—possibly with a battle-damaged airplane, certainly low on fuel and maybe wounded. Most of the German units operated from fields that were little more than commandeered farm meadows. Ulrich Steinhilper flew Messerschmitt 109s with the 1st Gruppe, JG 52, from such a field. "The mustiness of the tent and the dampness of the dawn were smells I well remember from those days at Coquelles, living in tents, British bell tents we had recovered from the beaches of Dunkirk. Pulling back the coarse army blankets I got up and felt the chill of the air, it was the end of September and already the dawn was cold. I washed and pulled on my uniform trousers and shirt, leaving off the collar—today as on most days I would be flying early and there was no place for the

formal collar and tie in the cockpit of my fighter. Although the army boys called us 'Die Schlippsoldaten' (the Necktie Soldiers) nobody with any experience flew in a collar and tie.

"Helmet Kuhle, the squadron leader, was suffering from blocked eustachian tubes in his inner ear and, as a result, he couldn't fly. He'd tried many times over the past few days, but as soon as we started to gain altitude the pain would become unbearable and he would have to break for home. So this morning, September thirtieth, I was to lead the small group which would represent our squadron—just four of us. Our gruppe had entered the Battle of Britain with thirty-six experienced pilots in three squadrons. Now there were just a handful left.

"For those who could eat prior to a flight there was food and hot coffee, but for many now breakfast consisted of a chain of cigarettes, each one lit from the butt of its predecesor. I hated the waiting. I could feel the acid bile building in my stomach and an awful nausea which seemed to wash through my whole body—nerves and accumulated battle fatigue. We had been flying day in and day out for weeks and the stress was beginning to show. More and more cases of 'Kanalkrankheit' (Channel sickness) were being reported and it was no wonder: A tour of duty for the bomber crews was twenty-five missions. By then we fighter pilots had flown over one hundred, the equivalent of four tours without a rest.

"How many flights would we make today? Eight was the most we'd managed in one day so far. Incredible. We were to fly as escorts again, in line with the new policy of total protection for the bombers, a policy which found no favor with the fighter squadrons. We felt we had proved

beyond all reasonable doubt that our machines were at their most effective in the Freie Jagd (free hunt), not shackled inflexibly to the lumbering bombers without even any means of communicating with them. But Hitler had become obsessed with the bombing of England in reprisal for attacks on German cities and so we were hobbled guarding our bombers.

"I walked out with the other three pilots along the line of aircraft, each one protected by straw bales and covered with camouflage netting. I arrived at Yellow Two, my aircraft, and ran my hand along the leading edge of the wing, easing the leading edge slat out to see if it functioned okay. I needn't have. Peter, my mechanic, would have checked her over thoroughly and I knew she was as ready as she could be. Walking around to the wingroot I looked at the sky and chatted with Peter as he helped me to strap on my equipment: life jacket, yellow sea-water dye container, life raft, but no pistol (earlier in the month we had been forbidden to carry sidearms). Apparently many airmen, alone and seasick in the Channel and at the limits of their endurance, had taken what our high command saw as the 'easy way out'—shooting themselves in the head, rather than slowly dying with stomach and lungs full of the Channel. Bending forward to attach the parachute harness straps I felt as though I would be sick, but I quickly straightened up, knowing the feeling would soon pass.

"Dropping down into the familiar surroundings of the cockpit, I fastened the harness straps which held me firmly in my seat. I performed the few checks necessary and waited as Peter wound the handle of the starter, feeling the aircraft gently rocking on its wheels as the flywheel gathered speed and energy. At the right moment I

The well-designed and efficient cockpit of the Focke Wulf Fw 190 fighter.

pulled the handle which would engage the starter and the big DB 601 turned a couple of times and then fired. In seconds the control panel was alive as the gauges began to register and climb to the normal readings. Warning lights winked out as the engine settled to a steady pace. My left hand firmly on the throttle, I finished the pre-takeoff checks and signaled Peter to pull the chocks away. I told myself I would feel all right in a few moments. I could see the others coming out to line up with me on my left and right. Then it was time to go. A last check either side of the huge cowling, a wriggle of the body to get comfortable in the straps, a feel of the rudder with each foot and a firm grip on the stick with the right hand.

"Easing the throttle lever forward in one smooth action was, and always will be, one of the most exhilarating feelings I have ever had.

'A firm boot' begins to press in the middle of the back and the pressure stays there as the aircraft accelerates faster than a sports car. I keep the stick well back to hold the tail wheel on the ground. The 109 has a tendency to yaw on the main wheels if the tail is raised too quickly. Keep her in a straight line with the rudder, maintaining a steady pressure on the rudder to counter the swing due to torque. Watch the ASI [air speed indicator] as we approach takeoff speed, then relax the stick a fraction, and as one movement, the tail rises as the main wheels leave the ground. Retract the gear and the indicator lights wink out—at last. As always, the nausea passes.

"Our Schwarm of four climbed away along the coast to where we are to meet with the bombers; Feldwebel Sigi Voss is my Rottenhund, with the second Rotte being led by

Karl Ruttger with Unteroffizier Kurt Wolf as his number two—four of five pilots who had survived a very sticky situation over London three days earlier. Because of this we were still in a confident mood and ready to take on anything. Maybe overconfident. As we crossed the Channel, we were released from the main formation to undertake a Freie Jagd. This couldn't have been better for us as we believed our tactics had been too timid and were hungry for the chance to vindicate our theory—and a little impetuous becaue of it.

"We crossed the Sussex coast at about 0930 hours (10:30 UK time) and having gained plenty of height, we spotted a squadron of Hurricanes climbing below us among other formations. They were flying in three vic formations in line astern, very orthodox by our standards. I judged that they must have been somewhat

inexperienced and decided to attack. Over the RT I gave instructions that I would attack the leading formation, Voss the next, Ruttger and Wolf the third. I was conscious that there were many other formations of enemy aircraft in the area, but we were hungry for action and thought that our height and speed would see us through unmolested.

"On my order, we dropped into the attack, picking up terrific speed in the dive and dropping below and behind the Hurricanes. We were able to hit them from slightly below with complete surprise. I gave the order 'Nach Angriff in Linkskurve sammeln' (After the attack, assemble in left curve). We were not sure exactly what happened. We think that one of the others pressed the transmission button at the same time as me, but the actual effect was that the first two words of my instructions

were cut off, leaving just the order 'In Linkskurve sammeln' (Assemble in left curve). I went on firing for a good few seconds, sweeping right through the vic formation, not realizing that the others were breaking off almost immediately. They were understandably annoyed that they hadn't been able to fully press home their attacks, particularly in light of our shared feelings about officers who apparently risked all to raise their own personal scores.

"There was little time to debate what had happened because some of the other enemy fighters had seen our attack and turned upon us with great fury. Our small formation was broken up with me and Voss making it home and Ruttger limping in alone a while later. I witnessed Wolf's fate, seeing him hit by numerous shells from an enemy fighter in a beam attack . . . almost invariably fatal because of the

lack of armor on our sides. His aircraft began to burn immediately. We had paid dearly, our only consolation being that we had hit the enemy very hard, myself claiming my fourth victory, albeit with little enthusiasm.

"The morning had certainly given me cause for reflection. I had let my own impetuosity and that of my young colleagues overcome common sense. We had attacked with good results which would certainly have been better had we not had the mix-up on the radio; but I'd seen Kurt Wolf shot down. I was sure that he'd been killed and his death was weighing heavily on my conscience. My managing to get all of our people back in the evening went some way in assuaging my feelings of guilt. It had been a mission which went badly wrong with serious losses for the Luftwaffe, hardly any of which were attributable to enemy action.

left: The crew of a Heinkel HE 111 bomber before a raid on London; below: Servicing an HE 111 on a German base in France during WWII.

"Another escort duty, tied to the bombers as their protection. Once more I was to lead, with four aircraft from the squadron. During the morning another machine had been fixed and we were able to replace the missing Kurt Wolf. Our brief was to assemble with squadrons from our Gruppen and others, to escort JU 88s to London, flying blind, high above the clouds, relying on their navigation. They were using the experimental 'Knickebein' radio beams and should have hit the target with great accuracy. We missed London completely, passing it somewhere to the left. It was almost certainly a case of the leading bomber flying down the beam on course, but missing the intersecting beam which was to warn him that he was almost on target.

"The whole bomber Gruppe (about thirty aircraft) flew on, and only turned for home when we had used about two thirds of our fuel. And even then they didn't take the shortest course, but set off in the direction of the Isle of Wight where the Channel is at its widest. We couldn't leave the bombers because they were being constantly harassed by enemy fighters, and so the object became to conserve fuel as much as possible. However, it isn't easy to fly straight and level and give proper protection [at the same time], so the precious fuel reserves were running low.

"The fighters held their positions and as we began to cross the Channel we could see that the bomber force was still intact. Now it became a matter of survival for the fighters. At last we could break away and I ordered my Schwarm to drop to sea level where the wind resistance was lower. We literally wave-hopped, hoping that our fuel gauges were wrong and that we would have enough to get to France. One after another our com-rades came on the radio to report that their red fuel-warning lights had come on. Below us we could see the gray, uninviting waters with waves running very high. We knew that if we tried to land the aircraft in such rough water, our chances of survival were slim. So, as fuel ran still lower the orders were to try to gain a little height and jump. At least this gave an improved chance of survival, although not much better.

"One after another the fighters plowed into the waves of the Channel or rose in a last desperate effort to gain height before the pilot bailed out. Our track across those wild waters became dotted with parachutes, pilots floating in their life jackets, and greasy oil slicks on the cold water showing where yet another 109 had ended its last dive. Our air-sea rescue people tried their best, but it was so hard to locate men in the high waves. Most that were located were already dead, victims of exposure or drowning. The next day I saw a secret memorandum which reported nineteen pilots drowned. Only two were recovered by the *Seenotflugkommando*.

"My group of four survived and just made it to Boulogne where we refueled. All along the coast near Boulogne we had seen 109s down in the fields and on the grass, some standing on their noses. Our losses had been huge, the penalty for having been chained to the bombers and for not being able to communicate with the bomber leader. When we four flew into Coquelles, the ground crews went wild with joy. They had written us off with the others and were pleased that we had made it back.

"By September thirtieth 1940, there were few of the original thirty-six pilots left in our Gruppe. The survivors who were still flying were under great stress. Each of us knew by

Heinkel bombers on a raid to a target in southern England in the summer of 1940.

a quick perusal of the casualty list that our time must come soon."

A month later, Ulrich Steinhilper was shot down over Kent. "Unfortunately, on this day I didn't have my new Yellow Four, which had an automatic pitch-control propeller . . . because the airplane was having an overhaul. But we had more planes than pilots, so I used my good old Yellow Two, which was a bit slower but had already earned me five victory stripes on the tail. Peter, my mechanic, was happy. His neglected favorite had another chance. 'Maybe, Herr Oberleutnant,' he said, 'you will be more fortunate with this one. With the new airplane you don't seem so lucky.' They were his last words as he closed the hood.

"We assembled over France with about fifty ME 109s, twenty of them carrying bombs to London in the fighter-bomber mode. We were to protect them. When their bombs were dropped we would turn together for home with the aim to get back to Calais as quickly as possible.

"Together with my *Rottenhund,* Feldwebel Lothar Schieverhofer, I

Oscar Boesch, an Fw 190 pilot of IV JG 3, before an escort mission.

was at the top right in the formation—the nucleus of it being the fighter-bombers. They flew in a tight formation, while for protection we flew at different heights and to the sides. Suddenly, one of our pilots, Rabe, shouted into the radio: 'Eleven o'clock high! Vapor trails. Same flight direction.' Yes, they were there. To the left and above, British fighters . . .

waiting in a higher and superior position. They were just biding their time for when we were in our weakest tactical situation. The two-fighter Rotte was designed [for mutual protection], but in a curve this was useless because while turning we could not protect each others' tails. Clearly, the moment to attack was when we turned for home. In the meantime, we just kept our eyes on them.

"From my position I had a pretty good view. It all looked quite attractive and peaceful, these white and silver condensation stripes, straight lines in the blue sky. But no time to admire vapor trails. I had problems. The old Yellow Two had been parked for days and during these cold October nights water must have collected in the propeller-pitch change mechanism. Now, at altitude, that water had frozen and locked it solid.

"The suburbs of London were below and it became imperative that I know soon whether we would make our turn to the left or the right. In the presence of the British fighters, and with my propeller problems, it was essential for Schieverhofer and me to be in the best position. Apparently the squadron commander had similar worries. 'Right or left turn?' he asked over the radio. The wing leader answered: 'After Bombs Away, turn right.' Excellent. This was just what I needed. I would be right at the inside of the turn and afterward would not be at the end. It was a relief because it is always the poorest rabbits who are shot by the hunters.

"Then, 'Bombs Gone,' we dived down with the fighter-bombers, but as we did so all hell broke loose. And, as usual, everyone was speaking and shouting into their radios at once so that nothing could be heard but a crazy whistling noise. This noise of interference really got on one's

nerves, but above it all, one pilot shouted 'My bomb is still on . . . please slow down.' An angry voice came back, 'Well, pull your emergency bomb lever.' After that, nothing. Just the whistling. But now what was going on? Below they started the turn . . . to the left! Terrible. I was now in a position well to the right of my Rottenhund, who had followed the radio chatter and cleverly chosen his position to the right of me. And now we were turning to the left.

"We'd had it. About four or five fighters dived toward Schieverhofer with a lot more speed than we had. 'Watch it,' I shouted, and made a protecting turn to shoot behind his tail. But what was he doing? Instead of a dive away, he turned toward me and started to shoot behind my tail. A quick look back and I saw why. It was just like a staircase of Spitfires which led right up into the sun. The first one already had eight little guns winking at me from its wings and I slammed the 109 into a steep dive. Scheiverhofer was on his own now and would have to fend for himself.

"Then, bang. My over-revving motor had caused the supercharger to explode and the control column shook. However, the airplane remained operational, though I would have to be careful. I was certainly losing oil from the damage and had to get lower for more engine power. I slipped into a milky soup of cloud, let the control go back a bit and right away shot up into the blue again. I was almost blinded by the sudden change in light and my compass was running wildly with all this stamping on the rudder pedals. I knew, though, that I was on the right course and so went back into the murk. At once I was through it again. Below was land and the Thames Estuary. So, even with all my terrible speed I hadn't got very far.

Preparing to escort Luftwaffe bombers on a raid to a target city in England in 1940.

"But then I couldn't believe my eyes. I was right in the middle of some Hurricanes flying in a loose formation in the same direction. I was slightly above them and they didn't see me. Quickly I switched on my Revi gunsight, but flying through the clouds had caused ice to collect on my windscreen and everything was distorted. I tore off my gloves to adjust the metal aiming piece and at the same time removed my oxygen mask. Now I knew real fear. With the mask off, my airplane smelled like a steam locomotive. A glance at the instruments . . . one hundred thirty degrees Celcius. I must have been hit in the radiator. Right away I forgot about shooting anyone else down and was just glad they hadn't seen me.

"I turned the ignition off and went into a glide, calling the ground radio station with my position and predicament. They heard me and alerted air-sea rescue. Good. Now I was down to five hundred meters. Near a little town below, light antiaircraft guns opened fire. So, ignition on again and get some height. Into the clouds. Here the engine was running okay, but the oil temperature was rising visibly. Once more ignition off and into a glide. Now I could see Pegwell Bay off Manston and radioed my position.

"Down to two hundred fifty meters and I had to switch on again in a hurry, but even at low revs the engine shrieked. It was metal against metal now. Maybe full throttle would help? Yes, that helped all right. The engine just stopped dead.

"I had to jump. First, I wanted to make a final radio statement. 'From Eule 2A. Engine has stopped. Am bailing out.' It was crazy how loud I sounded in the quietness around me. 'Poor Yellow Two. This is now your very last minute,' I said, tearing off my helmet, headset and mask. I pulled the hood lever but nothing happened and I couldn't move the handle another millimeter. Damn. At two hundred fifty meters and two hundred KMPH I had to get out quickly, so I pulled open the cabin roofing. With a rumble it flew off to the rear. Pushing up I was suddenly out into a storm, somersaulting past my fighter. After my escape I didn't care how many somersaults I did or which direction they were going . . . only to get the parachute open. I looked for the D-ring, pulled and a small silk thread came up between my legs.

"Incredibly, the drogue chute had wound itself around my leg and when the main chute opened it felt as if my leg had been torn off. The rearward tumbling stopped with a suddeness; then I was hanging by my left leg turning round and round as an axle. Finally, this also ended and I was in the right position. I could still move the leg but it was extremely painful. Just at that moment I saw my Yellow Two head straight into the soft-looking ground right in the middle of a herd of cows which were running off in all directions, their tails raised in the air. At once its ammunition started to go off—a kind of ridiculous salute of honor.

"Now I was lucky. Just at the end of a swing on my parachute, I landed quite gently on my right leg on the soft ground. For my injured left knee it couldn't have been better. Now I stood on English soil. The sky above was dark gray and a light drizzle fell. Down here it was hard to believe that moments earlier I had been floating up there in the brightness of the sun. One thing was certain. From now on, and for quite a long time, I would no longer be the master of my own fate. A feeling of hopelessness almost overwhelmed me and made me want to cry. Above I could hear the howling engines of my returning comrades with whom I had so recently been in radio contact. Now, how helplessly far away from them I was."

Though he might not have thought so at the time, Ulrich was a lucky man. He was, at least, alive. For his dwindling band of fellow airmen, survival was quite unlikely. The Battle of Britain was all but over, but the raids would go on into November and December. And those who got through 1940 on the Channel coast and then went on to the Eastern Front had an even slimmer chance of surviving the war. Captivity had its compensations.

In the camps, first in Britain and then in Canada, Ulrich was reunited with a number of old colleagues—men who had long since been written off as killed over England or the Channel. Kurt Wolf, whom Ulrich was sure had been killed, was there. Despite the fearsome attack on his Messerschmitt, Wolf had survived with a single bullet in his right leg and had parachuted down near Rye on the Sussex coast. For Ulrich it was wonderful to find that Kurt was alive. There too was his friend Schieverhofer. Shot down in the same combat with Ulrich, he had landed on the grass aerodrome at Penshurst, Kent. The victor, Pilot Officer Peter Chesters of 74 Squadron, had landed his Spitfire and taxied alongside to have the unique experience of taking his adversary prisoner.

In the four-month period of the Battle of Britain a total of 551 Luftwaffe fighter pilots were killed or taken prisoner.

There existed in the Luftwaffe what the RAF christened "Spitfire snobbery." It is now apparent that Hurricanes were the backbone of the

The German fighter ace Adolf Galland was credited with 104 aerial victories in WWII; right: Heinkel HE 111 bomber crewmen en route to England during the Battle of Britain.

RAF during the Battle of Britain and certainly accounted for the majority of German aircraft that were shot down or damaged. However, Luftwaffe pilots insisted that virtually everything they shot down was a Spitfire and invariably claimed to have been the victim of a Spitfire. This is well illustrated by an incident involving the late Robert Stanford-Tuck. Flying a Hurricane, he shot down a German fighter that fell close to Tuck's airfield. He promptly landed and jumped onto a truck that sped out to pick up the German pilot. As they arrived, the German was introduced to Tuck and he complimented him on the fighting capabilities of his Spitfire. Tuck explained that he had been flying a Hurricane but the German insisted that he'd been shot down by a Spitfire.

"We never thought we'd be beaten. We thought it might have gone on a bit longer. But the Battle of Britain as such . . . it stopped. We didn't win anything. I don't think we won any battles. But we did buy time . . . a little valuable time which enabled our Bomber Command to get ready. Don't forget, it's the only time in history two air fleets had ever met each other, and the change of a whole war happened. If we'd lost that air battle, you could have said the world today would be a different place."
—Flying Officer Dennis David

His fingers wake, and flutter up the bed. His eyes come open with a pull of will, helped by the yellow Mayflowers by his head. The blind-cord draws across the window-sill . . . What a smooth floor the ward has! What a rug! Who is that talking somewhere out of sight? Three flies are creeping round the shiny jug . . . 'Nurse! Doctor'/'Yes, all right, all right.'
—from *Conscious* by Wilfred Owen

When the pilots of the Debden-based 4th Fighter Group went to London on a 48-hour leave, they caught the 1:20 train from Audley End station near Saffron Walden.

TIME OUT OF WAR

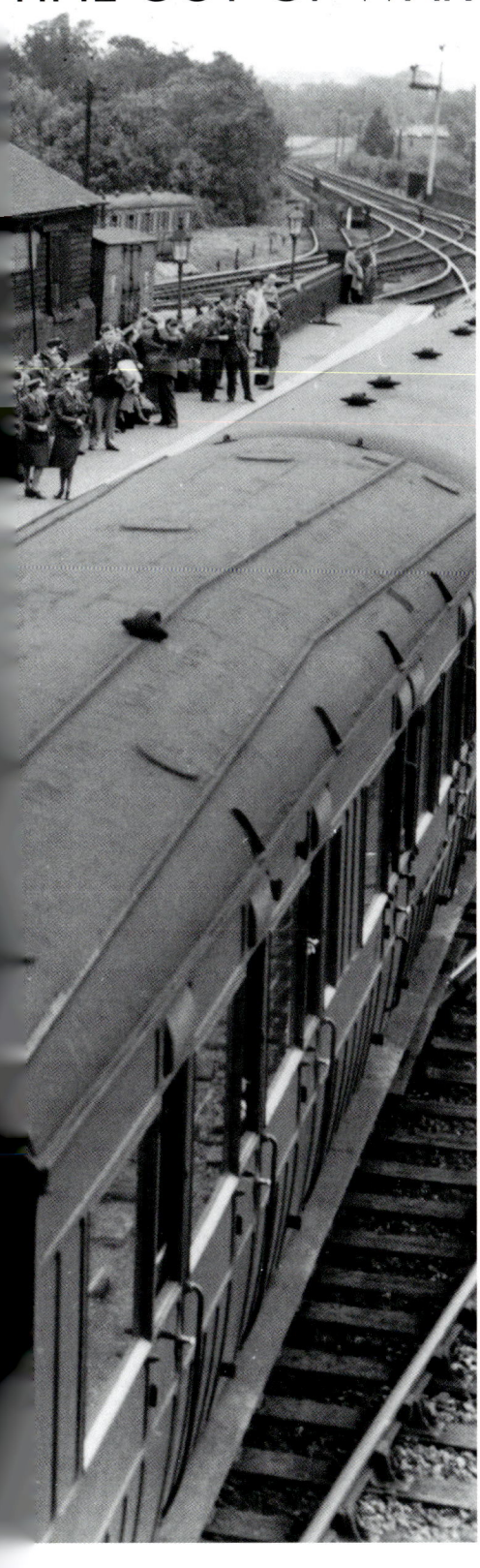

My candle burns at both ends; it will not last the night; but, ah, my foes, and, oh, my friends—it gives a lovely light.
—from *First Fig* by Edna St. Vincent Millay

The train was slowing down and we peered out the window to see what Audley End was like. Much to our dismay there was no town, just a railway station.
—from *The Look of Eagles* by John T. Godfrey

FOR THE ENGLISH PILOT "leave" usually meant time at home with his family, but for his American counterpart there could be no such comfort. Off duty, he would spend his time, money and emotion however it suited him . . . at liberty to enjoy himself on a "48." Home leave was something to be looked forward to only after a long tour of duty in England—he would have to try to unwind on occasional three-day passes to London or one of the other "liberty towns."

On base, the American could relax briefly in an officers' club or aero club, where he could read, have a beer, or play cards. Informal in furnishings and tone, these clubs were often given names by the pilots who used them; the Auger Inn, for example, at the 353rd Fighter Group's base near Raydon.

Sometimes, if lucky, a Yank would be befriended by a local family, welcomed and fed as one of their own. It was a unique experience for both guest and host. With few exceptions, these Americans had never before been outside their country, some never having crossed the border of their home state. Equally, many of their English hosts had never before met foreigners.

A forty-eight-hour pass was eagerly awaited by the American fighter pilot. It meant a time out of war and, often, a trip to London, where the action was. For the pilots of the East Wretham-based 359th Fighter Group, it was a fourteen-shilling round-trip adventure. One of them takes us along for the ride: "You stood on that train from Thetford all the way to London, your feet numb in the drafty corridor, the windows steamed so that even the bleak Suffolk landscape was hidden in the November curtain of cold. There was the jerking, stopping, backing, starting, and there was the inevitable twenty-minute stop at Ely. You cursed the heat lever over the seat. It never worked.

"But then it was April, a half year later. You left your overcoat in the belly-tank crate that served as a wall locker, stuffed some shaving articles in your musette bag, and hopped the five fifty or the nine or eleven o'clock bus from the gate. You were taking off on a forty-eight to London. It was spring and you felt eager.

"No tickets now at the fourteen-bob-the-round-trip rate. In April 1945, you began getting reverse lend-lease travel warrants to any point in the UK. You waited on the platform for the train to pull in from Norwich, buying a *Daily Express, Mail, Post, Sketch,* or *Illustrated.* Then you read the signs—THERE'LL ALWAYS BE MAZAWATTEE TEA—and watched a farmer herd two goats off the Bury train through the passengers. And you looked over the local civilians, the British officers and the scores of American airmen, a few of them with all their gear starting the trip back to the States. Local trains from Swaffam and Watton arrive with school kids in shorts and high wool stockings, clutching their books like school kids anywhere. Thetford is a small town, but its station carried life in and out by day and night: girls from Knettishall, Scottish officers in kilts, clean-shaven GIs starting on leave and returning ones unpressed, unshaven, and unwell.

"There was the morning a few months after D-Day when your train was an hour late and then you saw why. A hospital trained steamed in to pick up a score of U.S. wounded, casualties headed for the States. There was no ceremony. No coffee with doughnuts and brave smiles. The wounded just stared right back at those who stared at them, their eyes dull and tired . . .

"You sat in the compartment and slept most of the way. That is, you sat when there was a seat. One of the eight that could be crowded into each compartment. Opposite you was a minister who smiled in a kindly, professional way; three gunners from the B-17 field near Bury, invariably sleeping; two civilian women next to you reading a cheaply covered book and holding boxes and babies; a civilian smoking steadily, his pipe acrid and penetrating, tobacco shreds sprinkled unnoticed on his well-worn coat. You read the signs on the train: IF DANGER SEEMS IMMINENT, LIE ON THE FLOOR, advised the poster next to the watercolor of the cathedral. IT IS DANGEROUS FOR PASSENGERS TO PUT THEIR HEADS OUT OF THE CARRIAGE WINDOWS warned the message over the door with the window you opened by working a heavy leather strap.

"Italian POWs were standing and sitting around the freight cars at Brandon, smoking and waving, but mostly just watching and joking with each other. The civilian next to you explained that the land around Ely was all under water a long time ago, and that the cathedral was raised on the only high ground in the vicinity. You see planted fields slipping by. CARELESS TALK COSTS LIVES . . . You reach Cambridge and know your trip is two-thirds done, only two stops now and you'll be at Liverpool Street Station—London. The train picks up speed through the canals and pastures the other side of Cambridge and finally you pass the row houses, each with its vegetable garden facing the railroad track, an air raid shelter in the garden, and each with laundry out on the lines. Ten minutes now . . . You are up on an elevated track banked on both sides with the ruins and debris of bombed-out apartment houses, factories, churches, and office buildings. You know then you are in London.

"Liverpool Street Station . . . 'Tickets please.' The station is noisy with hissing steam from your train, the familiar voice of the girl announcer and the crowds of people heading for the tube. It is unlike any American train station, for there are no hilarious meetings or emotional good-byes. Everyone is intent upon his own journey; to the London man or woman the train is not a novelty, it is a God-sent chance to get away to the country for one night of solid sleep away from the bombs, V-1s and V-2s. To the GI arriving, the train is no novelty either. It has been a boring, uncomfortable means of getting to the city where he plans to stay awake . . .

"Your pass is almost up. You get to the station at eight o'clock and find a seat. Then you joke with the girl you met or brought along and maybe try a cup of scalding tea in the canteen. You're on the eight twenty. Now you find sleep easy, and you no longer have to keep your uniform pressed or clean. You are unshaven and tired, and you smoke and read the London papers . . . Lakenheath, Brandon, Thetford.

"Forty-eights to London were a little different each time you went. You remember some of the sights and sounds, and the flat English countryside divided by trees, hedges, and waterways. You will never forget the voice of the girl calling trains at Cambridge and the shafts of light cutting through the steam in Liverpool Street Station."

In London, the attractions were much the same for the serviceman as for any tourist—the Thames, the Houses of Parliament, St. Paul's, and Buckingham Palace all featured on the "places to go-things to do" list for the American aviator. Off the list, nightclubs were popular, the Washington, the Nuthouse, and the American Melody Club among the favorites. The American Eagle Club at 28 Charing Cross Road was a regular haunt of U.S. pilots. They often visited Rainbow Corner, the Red Cross—run club on Shaftesbury Avenue. Other attractions included the "Piccadilly Lilies" who plied their trade by day and night, targetting the well-paid American fliers with precision.

The American officer in London could take his meals at an exclusive eating house known as Willow Run. Located in the Grosvenor House Hotel, Willow Run provided the Yank with food that would make him feel at home and that he knew would surpass the stodgy, indifferent, and meager meals available in English restaurants. Pork chops, mashed potatoes, ice cream, sweet corn, pancakes, fried chicken and steak were offered—luxuries to help the Americans forget the frugality of wartime Britain. Featuring chefs—whose culinary careers had been postponed by the draft—from some of America's most interesting restaurants, the "Run" served delights from the menus of Boston's Kenmore, the El Paso Hilton, Rand's Bakehouse of Morgantown, West Virginia, and the Sabinal (Texas) Chicken Shack.

Another way to relax on R & R was at the large country houses that had been turned over to the U.S. Army Air Force for use as "rest homes." The Air Force understood the importance of such interludes in

The Americans brought the Jitterbug
to England in World War II.

A "rest home" for war-weary airmen was run by the American Red Cross near Salisbury; right: Coombe House, another such facility was located at Shaftsbury.

restoring war-weary fliers to combat-ready condition. One such facility was Broadlands at Romsey, the country home of Earl Mountbatten. Exhausted and flak-happy types were delivered by B-17s to nearby Stony Cross airfield for a week away from the battlefront. Coombe House, at Shaftesbury, was a rest home run by American Red Cross girls. One of them, Ann Newdick, wrote of her life at Coombe House—"the flak farm," as the American airmen called it: "It's January in England, so the morning sun is rare and welcome. Breakfast is bacon and eggs. Apparently the grapevine knew it too because half the house is up for breakfast, twenty or so combat fliers disguised in sweaters, slacks, and sneakers. Plans are afoot for golf, tennis, and shooting skeet in the backyard, but the loudest conversation and most uproarious kidding centers around the four who are

going to ride to the hounds in a country fox hunt. On a rainy day there's almost as much activity at Coombe House—the badminton court in the ballroom is our chief pride. But nevertheless, the Army calls it a Rest Home. It looks as English as the setting for a Noël Coward play, but even as you approach the house you discover that actors and plot are American. You meet a girl in scuffed saddle shoes and baggy sweater bicycling along a shaded drive with a dozen young men. You'd guess it was a co-ed's dream of a college house party—not a military post to which men are assigned and where girls are stationed to do a job. We have so much fun that we usually forget its military purpose, and so much the better, because this house party is a successful experiment to bring combat fliers back to the peak of their efficiency.

"There are four of us here,

below: American Air Force personnel on their base in Norfolk, England, selecting turkeys for their Thanksgiving dinner in November 1943; overleaf: A Red Cross-spondored picnic in London for USAAF airmen on leave.

American girls sent overseas by the Red Cross. Never in our wildest dreams did we expect such a job. At first we felt almost guilty to be having such a good time. I was talking about what a picnic it was to one of the boys. 'That's the way it should be,' he said with authority. When I looked again I remembered that he was a medical officer who'd been at Coombe for about six weeks. In our conversation, I found out that he was Captain David Wright, Psychiatric Consultant for the Eighth Air Force. He had spent his six weeks in careful observation to decide the value of Rest Homes. 'Coombe House and the others like it,' he said, 'represent the best work of preventive medicine in the ETO. Very definitely Rest Homes are saving lives—and badly needed airmen—by returning men to combat as more efficient fliers.' A remarkable percentage of men who finish their tours have had a chance to be in Rest Homes sometime during their combat tour. There isn't any one word to describe the varying states of mind of combat fliers when they are just plain tired. Tired because it's hard work flying a P-38 or navigating a B-24 or shooting out of the waist window of a Fort. Tired as anyone is after intense mental and muscular strain—intermittent though it is, the lulls in between are not long enough for the flier to get past the let-down stage before he plunges into danger again.

"At first the Air Force ran these Rest Homes alone. After two had been established, a large part of the responsibility was transferred to the American Red Cross to make them as un-military as possible. The army Quartermaster outdoes itself on food, and 'Cooky' in the kitchen does it to perfection. Fried chicken, steaks, eggs, and ice cream are regular items on the menu, all served by pretty wait-

resses. 'Irish Mike' and Cooky, and all the rest of them are contributions of the Red Cross, which disguise the technical and military nature of Coombe House almost beyond recognition, and we four American girls show no obvious solicitude for anyone's morale. We turn down an invitation to play bridge if we want to dance with someone else. Lack of Army demands and freedom from regulations help create the free and easy tempo of the place. The whole feeling is one of such warmth and such sincerity that men come away knowing they have shared an experience of real and genuine living."

Rest homes and 48s were in stark contrast to the experience of the RAF fighter pilot. As one wife put it: "My husband could have been up at twenty thousand feet in the morning fighting the Germans . . . then home to lunch with me. It was almost unreal." While this nearly-cozy "home for tea" war in which the RAF operated in 1940 and 1941 may have helped their morale in a limited way, they too needed to unwind occasionally, at parties, pub crawls, clubs, and shows. It was the same for all airmen—they all needed to let off steam in a variety of outlets on and around the RAF fighter stations. One such was a "tradition" devised by Squadron Leader Geoff Warnes of 263 Squadron: a weekly "thrash." Believing in the value of such off-the-base gatherings for keeping a good squadron spirit, Warnes made Friday-night attendance compulsory for his pilots. The venue was the Golden Lion in Weymouth and no excuses for absence were accepted. On one occasion, a Flight Sergeant Proctor failed to appear and was hauled before his CO the next morning to explain himself. He thought he had a good enough reason for being absent—a date with a

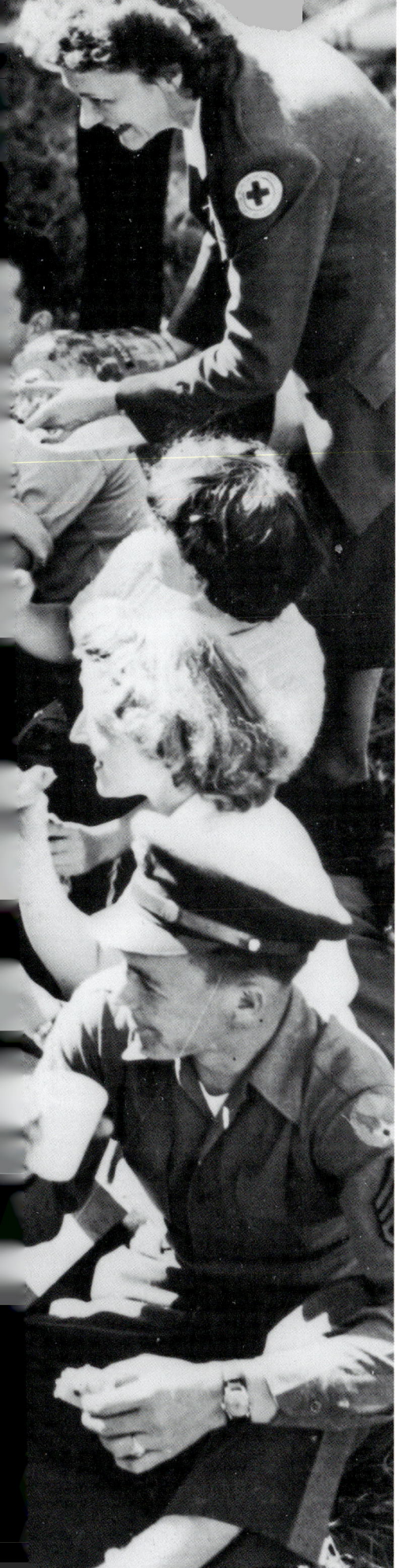

WAAF and a visit to the local cinema. Warnes was incensed. Women, Proctor was told, had two places—in the bedroom and the kitchen. Never, repeat never, were they to interfere with the Squadron Night Out. In future, he would be present on Friday nights. For Proctor, it was the end of a romance before it had begun. But Warnes's embargo aside, the women of the Auxiliary Air Force were part of the on-and-off duty lives of the RAF. Sergeant Dennis Todd, another 263 Squadron pilot, described his experience: "I had been changing some equipment at Stores when a WAAF officer appeared. 'Don't you salute officers, Sergeant?' she snapped. 'I'm not wearing my cap, Ma'am,' I said. 'Put it on and salute in the proper manner,' she demanded. I did so only to be ordered to give her my name and squadron number. No sooner had I got back to dispersal than Warnes called me to his office. A mild ticking-off then followed, with him confiding that he really didn't agree with the existence of 'Petticoat Bosses,' but [that] we had to tolerate them all the same. The following week the squadron was at a dance in one of the seafront hotels at Weymouth and one of the bedrooms had been turned over to us for a cloakroom. Sometime during the evening I realized that I had left my handkerchief in my greatcoat and went to the room to collect it. I opened the door and switched on the light. Then I heard something and realized I was not alone. Going round the end of the bed, I discovered there on the floor a Canadian pilot and 'my WAAF' in a very embarrassing situation. But I didn't salute. I didn't have my hat on and, in any case, she was improperly dressed."

Todd remembered another incident at Warmwell: "A pair of WAAF's knickers [black, elasticated bloomers,

often referred to as Blackouts, Passion Killers, or Wrist Breakers] were put to use on the airfield as a windsock until, one day, when a signal came in from Fighter Command to '. . . take down the WAAF's knickers.'"

Every squadron had its favorite local pub. Today, many of these places survive and are famous for their wartime associations. They are remembered and sought out by returning veterans. One of the most famous is the White Hart, at Brasted, which was frequented by Biggin Hill pilots during the war. Officers and other ranks would use separate pubs. At Biggin Hill, officers went to the White Hart; NCOs and airmen preferred the Jail in Jailhouse Lane. A favorite for Tangmere pilots was the Unicorn in Chichester. They also crowded a waterside establishment at Bosham called the Ship. The men at Hornchurch patronized the Good Intent. At North Weald it was the Crown in Epping, and at Fowlmere, the Chequers. Each pub had its own character, an ambiance in which the pilots felt comfortable and relaxed. The Yanks also enjoyed what was for them a new experience, English pub life.

Fighter pilots spent much of their leave time in England's pubs and clubs, and memories of them abound. One evening a group of 92 Squadron pilots were at the White Hart celebrating Biggin Hill's one-thousandth. They were warned by the village policeman that they were drinking after hours and must leave. The pilots then carried the lawman into the street and dumped him there. They filled his helmet with beer and wouldn't let him go until he had drunk it all. Surrounded by a dozen fighter boys he had little choice.

Some fighter pilots spent their leisure time as if there was no tomorrow. For many, there wasn't.

A dance held in a tent put up in front of the officer's mess at the Debden base of the 4th Fighter Group.

It isn't always being fast or accurate that counts; it's being willing. I found out early that most men, regardless of cause or need, aren't willing. They blink an eye or draw a breath before they pull a trigger. I won't.
—John Bernard Books in *The Shootist*

THERE WERE LEGENDS like Blakeslee, Gentile, Bader, Tuck, and Townsend. And there were other high achievers who were virtually unknown. Some of them shunned publicity and attention. Others died or were killed before the spotlight of fame could focus on their accomplishments. Either way, what did it take to be a successful fighter pilot?

Certain attributes were essential: motivation, aggressiveness, good eyesight, airmanship, and the ability to shoot straight. One fighter pilot commented on the importance of airmanship: "It's like a cavalryman making a charge on his horse. Is it horsemanship or fighting? Well, it's no good falling off the horse; that's for sure." And Derek Gilpin-Barnes, an intelligence officer wrote: "When you are with him, you find that the 'hero' is a myth. He is armed with no callous disregard of life and death. He is not fortified with some peculiar tough-ness of the body or spirit. Behind the glamour of their daring and devotion lie their personalities which, to my thinking, are more fascinating still. Nor do their great deeds lose in stature if we regard them as performed, not by heroes, but by ordinary men. The fighter pilot then, is an ordinary man . . . as scared of death as the next."

As leader of the 328th Fighter Squadron, 352nd Fighter Group, at Bodney, and as the third-highest-scor-ing American ace in England, George Preddy was perceived as a flamboyant pilot who fought and played hard, and enjoyed the life of a fighter pilot. In this, he conformed to the stereo-typical media image. What didn't fit was the sensitive side of his nature, his penchant for writing poetry, and a deep love of family life. For such a high scorer, he is relatively unknown. In fact, the journal of the American Aviation Historical Society once described him as "the unknown ace." Preddy did not ultimately fall victim to the guns of the Luftwaffe. Instead, in a tragic blunder, he was shot from the sky by U.S. Army antiaircraft fire near Koblenz on Christmas Day, 1944.

The highly successful Carroll "Red" McColpin returned to the United States at one point in the war to help train and form new fighter groups. During his stay, he was asked by General "Hap" Arnold "What is the best bomber we've got?" "Sir," replied McColpin, "I think the P-38 is the best bomber." "God, he got mad." McColpin recalled. "Why do you say that?" Arnold asked. "Well, it's got two engines instead of four. It carries two thousand-pounders. Only got one guy in it instead of ten, so if you lose one, it's a lot cheaper on people . . . and also, a fighter pilot in a P-38, if you wanted to send him in to bomb some-thing with two thousand-pounders, can probably hit the target most of the time . . . and the bombers can't."

Pilot Officer Roger Hall flew Spitfires with No 152 Squadron at Warmwell, Dorset. "We all had to suppress fear for obvious reasons; not least was the desire to appear without it and so retain your own self-respect, for having lost this we were on the way down.

"September 17, 1942, was the day when I made my last operational flight. I had passed the point of no return. I was no longer consciously tired. I was an inanimate being actuated only by automatic reflexes. I kept very much to myself and the death wish began to dominate my mind. I was a totally irresponsible agent, but I seemed to

left: Aces of the 56th Fighter Group, 8AF, left to right, Bob Johnson, Hub Zemke, and Bud Mahurin; below: Mahurin in 1990.

B-17Gs of the Horham-based 95th Bomb
Group with their escort of P-47 Thunderbolts.

have acquired a sort of second wind. An unnatural abundance of energy flowed through me and I knew that, if once I let go, I should flounder totally and never recover again, so great would be the reaction. We had only four pilots in the flight now and we had to be at readiness in our cockpits because the German recce planes and low-level fighter-bombers were coming in low over the sea, undetected by radar and inflicting damage on the coastal districts.

"Pilots in pairs spent an hour at a time at cockpit readiness and then they were relieved by the other two. We tried to read a magazine or a book or the paper at these times though it wasn't easy. Tension was about you all the time, especially when the hands of your watch crept toward the hour when you were due to be relieved. At about five minutes to the hour two reliefs would come out of the hut, carrying their helmets and taking the last few puffs of their cigarettes, and you wondered whether they would reach their machines before the alarm bell sounded for takeoff. If they did not, you knew damned well that you would have to go yourself."

The Air Force Cross was authorized by Congress in July 1960. It is the USAF equivalent of the U.S. Army's Distinguished Service Cross and the Navy Cross, all three medals ranking second only to the Medal of Honor, the highest American award for gallantry in combat. There have been two retrospective awards of the Air Force Cross for acts of valor in World War II combat that were not recognized at the time. Lieutenant Urban Drew was one of the most successful fighter pilots in the 361st Fighter Group when, on October 8, 1944, he bounced two Messerschmitt

ME 262s on returning from an escort mission to Czechoslovakia. Drew spotted the two aircraft taking off from Achmer and, leaving his deputy squadron leader in charge, rolled into a near vertical dive with his number two and number three aircraft, firing as he pulled out. One of the ME 262s exploded instantly with such ferocity that Drew's Mustang was thrown about by the blast. The second 262 broke left in a steep climbing turn to escape fthe P-51s. Drew's official report of the action: "I was still indicating about 400 mph and I had to haul back on the stick to stay with him. I started shooting from about sixty degrees deflection, 300 yards, and my bullets were just hitting the tail section of the enemy aircraft. I kept horsing back on the stick and my bullets crept up the fuselage to the cockpit . . . I saw the canopy go flying off . . . and the plane rolled over . . . hitting the ground at about a sixty degree angle."

Drew knew without doubt, that he had destroyed two ME 262 fighters, but he couldn't prove it. His gun camera had jammed and his number two who could have confirmed the kills, had been shot down by flak. His number three had broken away to the right and had seen only two columns of smoke and not the actual shooting down. There was insufficient evidence to support the recommended award of the Distinguished Service Cross for Drew. Years after the event, German records confirmed that Lieutenant Drew had indeed destroyed the two ME 262s. His claim had been justified. The Air Force Board for the Correction of Military Records reviewed the case and, subsequently, recommended that Drew be awarded the Air Force Cross (which had superseded the DSC). In May 1983, Drew—now a retired major—was presented with his medal in Washington by Air Force Secretary Verne Orr.

Flying Officer E. J. "Cobber" Kain was the first Allied ace of the war. Inevitably, he was pursued by the press. Eager for a real-life hero for their readers, the war correspondents chased this twenty-one-year-old New Zealander relentlessly. Noel Monks of the London *Daily Mail* was quick to recognize the possibilities in Kain, whom he described as " . . . an officer and a gentleman." Newspaper editors believed that their readers expected their heroes to be larger than life. As ordinary men, the fighter pilots might not have captured the public imagination. They had to be dashing, romantic, good-looking, extroverted . . . and far from "ordinary." Fortunately, Kain made good copy.

Kain was first rejected as an RAF recruit, which made him an even better story. That he had come from faraway New Zealand added to his appeal and that he also happened to be very good-looking was even more intriguing than his ability as a pilot and brilliance as a marksman. He was the leading ace and personality during the Battle of France. By the early spring of 1940, Kain had destroyed seventeen German aircraft, was shot down twice and had been awarded the DFC. He appeared constantly in the newspapers until, in a change of policy, the authorities censored the use of pilots' names in order to discourage the creation of individual heroes. Overnight, "Cobber" Kain, the hero, became "a twenty-one-year-old New Zealander." Then, recalled to England for training duties, he performed one last spirited beat-up of his French base. He misjudged a series of rolls and cartwheeled across the airfield. Kain the hero was dead; the fight-

er-pilot stereotype had been born.

An older man who led an American fighter group into action, Hubert "Hub" Zemke was thirty when he took the 56th Fighter Group to war over Europe. Zemke was driven by a zealous and aggressive urge for combat. This tenacious man led the organization known as "Zemke's Wolfpack." He exhorted his men: "A fighter pilot must possess an inner urge for combat. The will at all times to be offensive will develop into his own tactics. I stay with an enemy until either he's destroyed, I'm out of ammunition, he evades into the clouds, I'm driven off, or I'm too low on gasoline to continue the combat."

This philosphy had its effect on the Wolfpack's pilots, as shown by the kill scores of Francis Gabreski, Walker Mahurin, Dave Schilling, and Bob Johnson, all of them high-scoring aces. Bob Johnson accrued twenty-eight victories, becoming the first American pilot to exceed the World War I score of twenty-six by Eddie Rickenbacker. Johnson advised new pilots: "If he comes down on you, pull up into him and nine times out of ten, if you are nearly head-on with him, he'll roll away to his right. Then you have him. Roll onto his tail and go get him."

Similar advice was given by Don Blakeslee of the 4th Fighter Group. The pilots he led became known as the "Blakesleewaffe." He told his men that they should turn head-on into an attack and under no circumstances whatsoever should they deviate from this course of action. In a briefing, one young lieutenant timidly enquired, "But Colonel, what if the German doesn't break either?" With an icy stare, Blakeslee answered, "Then, sonny, you will have just earned your hazardous duty pay."

John McAdam, a shy young

4th Fighter Group pilots, top left: Pierce McKennon, top right: Winslow "Mike" Sobanski, below: Vermont Garrison, and left: Don Blakeslee, group commander of the 4th.

Ulsterman, was the epitome of Gilpin-Barnes's "ordinary man." Yet, as a sergeant pilot flying Spitfires with 41 Squadron during the Battle of Britain, he formed part of the backbone of the RAF's defense force. He is remembered by one who knew him as "small in stature, but a giant when it came to courage." Norman Ryder, the acting CO of 41, did his best to protect McAdam, but he had difficulty flying in formation at high altitude and was very vulnerable. Ryder sent him on leave the first time he was shot down.

During that home leave, McAdam had spent time in a local quarry firing his Browning pistol. The experience of being shot down had shaken him and he practiced firing that pistol until he could do it without flinching. He wrote home of his experiences: "Dear Pop, Yesterday, as you know, was a big day for the Air Force. We had been up four or five times in the morning to tame one or two recce machines, but I was not too happy because my engine was running very roughly. I still had the old 'floater,' EB-F. Anyway, the raid came over and we went up. I got left behind in the main chase and so I climbed to about 20,000 feet and saw below a ME 109. From the way he went down I presume he never knew what hit him. Then I saw another of our squadron and we flew parallel about a hundred yards apart and watching each others' tails. We flew over to the center of the city above the balloons, when I saw a lot of AA fire to the east of us. In a second or two I saw about five hundred bombers with a strong fighter escort above them and told my companion that I was going to investigate if he would watch my tail. Climbing up very carefully, I saw that there were many separate squadrons at different levels. I chose a squadron that was about thirty-five or forty strong and in line-astern. I dived on the tail of the last one. He burst into flames and I followed him down. When I was sure he was gone I zoomed up into a loop and dived down on the next in line of the squadron. By this time my machine was like a sieve with oil and glycol pouring out. However, I got the next one and as I followed him down the next of his squadron opened fire on me with a nice line in cross-fire, in addition to which I had a few other 109s and 110s chasing me. All my ammunition was gone and the plane was hardly moving. I thanked my lucky stars I had practiced my aerobatics to perfection, did a loop, rolled off the top of it, and looped again until I shook them all off. All this time the glycol was spewing out of the nose of the plane and the radiator temperature dropped back to zero, the

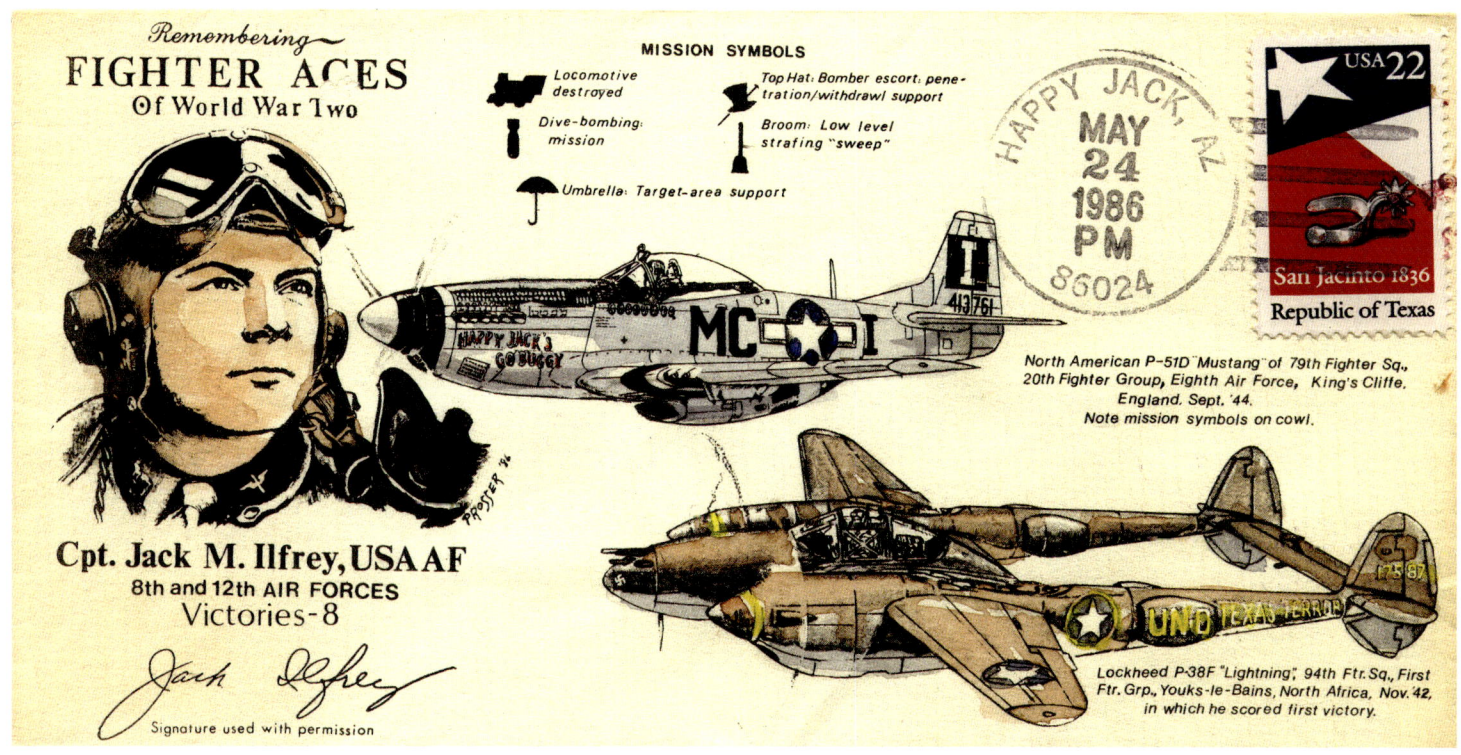

Remembering FIGHTER ACES Of World War Two

MISSION SYMBOLS

Locomotive destroyed

Dive-bombing mission

Umbrella: Target-area support

Top Hat: Bomber escort: penetration/withdrawl support

Broom: Low level strafing "sweep"

Cpt. Jack M. Ilfrey, USA AF 8th and 12th AIR FORCES Victories-8

Signature used with permission

North American P-51D "Mustang" of 79th Fighter Sq., 20th Fighter Group, Eighth Air Force, King's Cliffe. England. Sept. '44. Note mission symbols on cowl.

Lockheed P-38F "Lightning", 94th Ftr. Sq., First Ftr. Grp., Youks-le-Bains, North Africa, Nov. 42. in which he scored first victory.

oil temperature went up and finally off the clock. Then, of course, a ME 109 came to play with me, so I had to do something to discourage him. I pulled the stick straight back and put full right rudder on and the plane went into a spin. I let it spin about three times and then pulled out very carefully because the machine was full of holes and not too strong. This didn't shake the 109 off and he came at me again. I trimmed the plane for a right-hand gliding turn, lowered my seat, pulled my knees up and head down and took full advantage of the armour plate behind me. I heard about ten or twelve bullets hitting the plating and then miracle number one happened. Sergeant Darling, my companion over the city, came along and with his last burst hit the 109 for six, and I continued on my way. The engine, by this time, was out of glycol and red hot. It seized and just stopped.

The oil sprayed on the hot engine and burst into flames. I looked around for a place to land but all I could see was houses. I was going to jump for it but did not have enough height.

"At last I found a field and glided towards it in a sideslip to keep the flames away from the cockpit. I tried to lower the flaps and slow down but it was no use. When I thought I was about forty feet up (I couldn't see anything because of the smoke) I pulled the stick right back, hit tail first and pancaked onto the ground. I went through a couple of walls and a few trees, cartwheeled over twice and finally came to rest upside-down with me inside, unhurt. That was miracle number two.

"It was getting rather hot inside and I was unable to get out. I was just going to shoot myself to get it over with when a man came along with an axe and split the side of the

cockpit open and pulled me out. I was escorted into a house and, of course, was the centre of attention for miles around. At last a police-man came around and fixed me up with transport back to base, so that was more or less that. I have a few scrapes and bruises but nothing broken and otherwise quite fit.
"Yours, John
"p.s. I wangled a new uniform and flying kit out of this performance."

Walker "Bud" Mahurin was a member of Hub Zemke's Wolfpack, flying P-47 Thunderbolts from their Halesworth base in Norfolk. "We had been grounded from operations for a week or so because of weather. When that happened we usually liked to fly the planes because they had a tendency to get sickness in the radios and what-not. I was up flying around the base and at the time my Jug had a great big

A B-17 bomber and two Mustang escort fighters, excellent warbird restorations in an air show over Duxford Airfield, Cambridgeshire; left: A postal cover honoring the fighter aces of World War II.

'bathtub' external fuel tank prior to us getting the more aerodynamic tanks. I saw a B-24 flying along at low altitude and flew formation with it. They waved and I waved and the waist gunner waved and the pilots were waving—boyish enthusiasm, I guess. We passed right over our base at probably about a thousand feet, maybe twelve hundred feet, and I had to lower flaps in order to stay with them. I got pretty close and, when it came time to leave, I dropped down below the B-24 wing and increased the throttle and started to go forward. The crew in the 24 were watching me. I tried to descend by pushing the stick forward, but the tail of my airplane kept going up and it finally was sucked into the propellers on the starboard side . . . and I suddenly felt the stick go limp, and I knew instantly what had happened and bailed out right away. The B-24 guys feathered two engines on that side and eventually made a successful landing. They thought it was a big joke . . . but, of course, it bothered the hell out of me. I'll never forget driving back onto the base, sittin' in the back of the jeep with this huge parachute in my arms, billowing in the wind, wondering what in the hell was gonna happen to me now."

One of the first American fighter pilots in Britain in the Second World War was Leo Nomis, a member of No 71 (Eagle) Squadron, who remained in the Royal Air Force for the duration of the war. He remembered a certain unauthorized trip he made to France. "I was supposed to be doing an aircraft test. In those days you had to fly way the hell down around the estuary because they had a big balloon barrage, so I got down past Dungeness and started to cross the Channel. It seemed like I was on a rail, like a train. I just kept heading for Calais, the worst

place you could head for—the worst place you could go—at sea level. I was about a hundred feet off the water to keep out of the radar. Had no idea what I was going to do and actually had no idea why. But, the closer I got, the closer Calais was coming so I just kept flying straight at it. I finally got up to the beach and it looked like it had barbed wire and God knows what . . . all kinds of obstacles, and there was a whole bunch of buildings right behind it. Not a peep out of 'em. Nothing out of them yet. Maybe they were still trying to figure out whether I had one radiator or two. A lot of guys got fooled with those 109s that way. They'd wait until they could count the radiators, and it was too late. There was just a great big building . . . I didn't know what it was, and I just started firing the cannon and machine guns straight at it. If there were guys sleeping in there, they really had a helluva surprise. I just applied all the cannon and damned near hit the building when I pulled up, and then I turned so tight I almost blacked out. This was still less than a hundred feet off the ground. Then I was heading down and there was what looked like a great big sentry box with a bunch of apparatus on top of it. So, I started to fire at it and I missed it altogether. This was still with the machine guns. I'd fired all the cannon ammo at whatever in the hell that big place was . . . and they were bouncing off and ricocheting all over . . . you could see them hitting the dust.

"I was just leisurely trying to fly out and all of a sudden I heard two muffled reports and there were two big black puffs, one under and one on the other side of the wing. They were shooting 88mm straight trajectory and then a whole carload of Bofors stuff started to come. I was still fifty feet up, just crossing the beach . . . and it startled me so much I made

A Luftwaffe fighter pilot climbing into his Fw 190 during the final defense of the Reich late in the war.

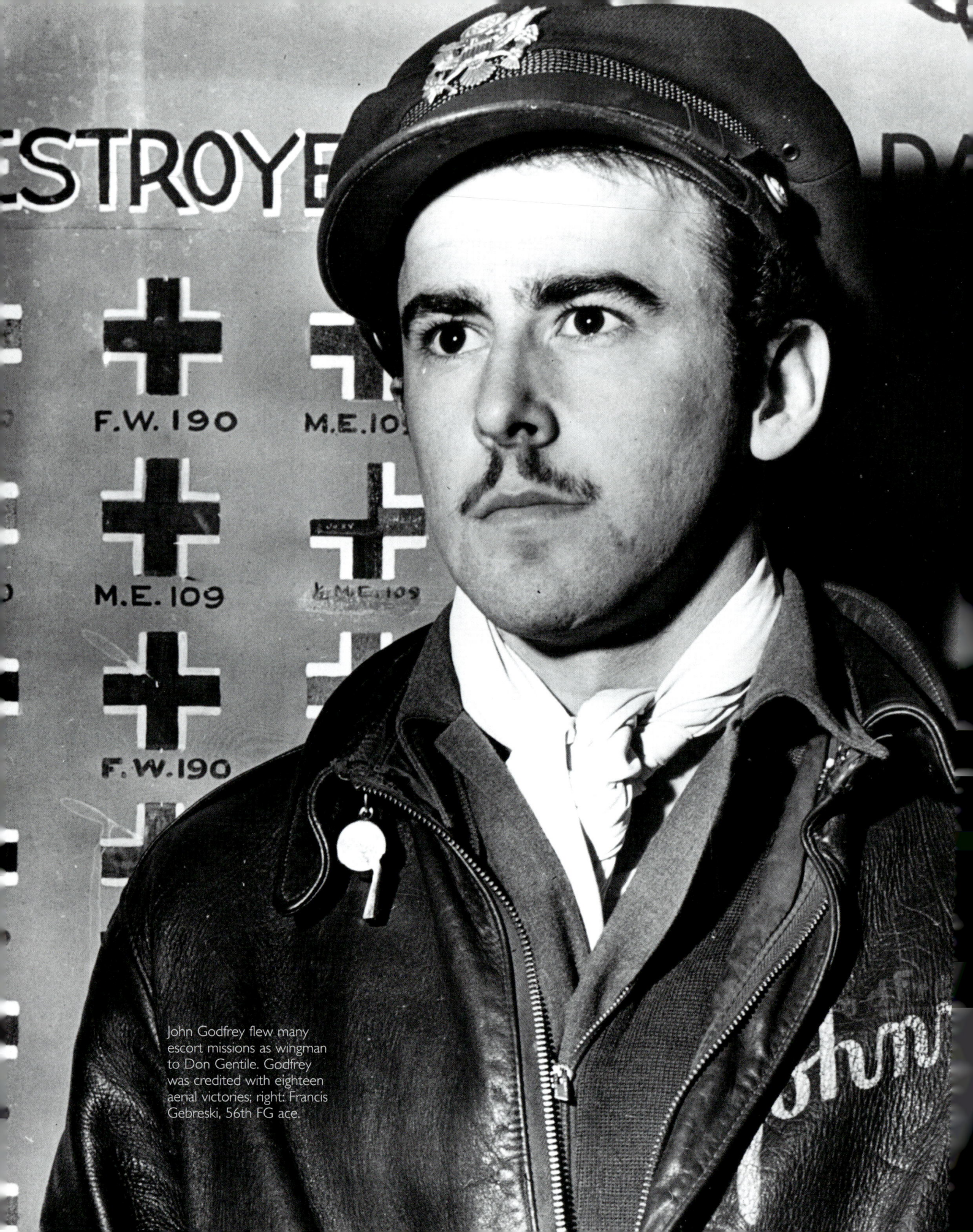

John Godfrey flew many escort missions as wingman to Don Gentile. Godfrey was credited with eighteen aerial victories; right: Francis Gebreski, 56th FG ace.

a three-hundred-sixty-degree tight turn and almost blacked out again. I went back in, and all this stuff was going out. This is what saved me. If I'd gone straight on, they couldn't have missed. I looked behind me and it was a whole mass of black puffs plus Bofors going everywhere . . . machine guns and whatever. I knew I had to get the hell out so I made another turn the same way only farther south. I was whipping back and forth as fast as I could and had everything pushed forward and was just about out over the water and was going about 305 mph, which was pretty good for a Spitfire, and they were still getting pretty close. What they were doing was shooting ahead of me into the water and throwing spouts up. Only thing I could do was whip it back and forth. At that speed it took me out of range, and then half way across, they quit. They let up. They'd hit me. Only reason I knew they'd hit me was I looked down at where the rivets were on the wing over the wheel well, and there was a hole—a small hole but jagged and right where the tire was, so I knew there had to be a flat tire. I came back and when I came in—we were at Debden then—I radioed that I thought I had a flat tire. I just assumed this, in case I ground-looped or went over on my back. I didn't know what the hell was gonna happen, but I landed with the wheels down. I just swung a little bit to the right. I straightened out and no problem at all. The mechanics asked if everything was all right. I said, 'Yeah, fine . . . I got a flat tire' (they could see that). One of them had eyes as big as silver dollars and said I had a great bloody hole in that wheel well. A piece of shrapnel had come through and missed the radiator by only a bit, about an inch. Needless to say, they called Petersen. Robbie

Robinson, our intelligence officer, asked what happened. I said it was an aircraft test and I went and flew over Calais. It turned out to be a real problem because they were planning a raid at the time and they didn't want anybody going over certain areas. They'd even painted the planes up different just for that . . . put them white-washed white stripes on them. They didn't want it to leak out. Say, you went over there and had to crash-land. The Germans would say, 'What the hell are these white stripes? They're not usually like that. Something must be up.' So, Petersen had to shut it up. He didn't report it. There was no flight. He raised holy hell with me. But he couldn't court-martial me. So they confiscated the cine gun film and I was confined to quarters for a couple of weeks."

Obviously, not all fighter pilots could be aces. The vast majority never claimed anything more than a "probable," if that. Some got no further than their first day of operational duty. Pilot Officer Tommy Rose-Price joined 501 Squadron at Gravesend, fresh from training, on September 2, 1940, and was sent straight into combat with his Hurricane. Somewhere over Kent the Messerschmitts picked him off and no trace of him or his aircraft were ever found. As his commanding officer wrote a letter of condolence to the family, Rose-Price's car sat parked outside the watch office, still piled high with his unpacked gear. One squadron commander called such losses "the slaughter of the innocents."

A little curly-headed, good-for-nothing, and mischief-making monkey from his birth.
—from *Don Juan* by George Gordon, Lord Byron

Noise proves nothing. Often a hen who has merely laid an egg cackles as if she laid an asteroid.
—Samuel Clemens

A friend is one who dislikes the same people that you dislike.
—anonymous

Airman, down to earth, painting the
town red, swingbands merely enlarge
the hollow singing in your head.
—from *Song* by Gordon Symes

IT'S LIKE WEARING YOUR PLANE, said pilots
about the leather flying jacket that
General "Hap" Arnold had once dis-
missed with the remark: "Get something better." But to the pilots of the
U.S. Army Air Force in the Second
World War, there was nothing better. The A2 was a simple design that
was improved over the years to make
it more practical. Although the jacket
was made from thick, tough steerhide, horsehide, or goatskin, its lining
was only thin cotton. There was also
a lack of pockets—there were only
two on the front with vertical entries
and they held little more than a few
small pieces of paper, a candy bar,
and a pack of cigarettes.

Some officers had specially added
non-regulation side-entry pockets,
which were located behind the official front ones. The jacket was, however, a part of the serviceman's uniform, complying to strict government
specifications, and any personal alter-
ation was forbidden, though painted embellishments were tolerated.
Squadron patches and rank markings
were officially acceptable.

The A2 was a "windcheater,"
developed from the design of its
predecessor, the A1, which had
been a favorite jacket of aviation pio-
neers Charles Lindbergh and Jimmy
Doolittle. Though not perfect, the
A2 was a good, all-purpose garment.
Airmen felt comfortable in it. With a
full-length front zipper that fastened
up to the collar, knitted wool cuffs and
waistband, it kept the wind out and
the edge off cold temperatures. It was,
after all, designated as an intermediate
summer-weight jacket and if it had
had a warmer lining it would not have

Fighter and bomber pilots
of the American Air Force
stationed in Britain during
the Second World War
were proud and privileged
to wear the handsome and
practical A2 leather jacket.
Many of them decorated it
to their taste. This example
represents the airplane he
flew with the 401st Bomb
Group at Deenethorpe.

been so versatile. When temperatures were so low that the A2 no longer offered reasonable protecion, airmen wore a shearling-lined jacket, the B3.

The A2 design was finally standardized on May 9, 1931, and the army went shopping for suitable manufacturers to produce the garment. It was thought that sportswear makers would be appropriate as they would have the know-how and the necessary machinery to do the job. Manufacturers of shoes, raincoats, and outerwear were used as well. They were contracted to produce a given number of garments and then were sent the approved government specifications so that patterns could be drawn up. Although the manufacturers had to strictly adhere to the design, each had their own house style. For example, there were differences in the curvature of pocket flaps and in collar points, and in the shade of brown used to dye the leather. Even the sizes varied from maker to maker. An Aero Leather size 40 was considerably

larger than a Perry Sportswear size 40.

The orginal specs required that the A2 be made from three-ounce horsehide in the color of Seal Brown, quite a dark brown with a reddish tint. By the beginning of World War II, demand for the garment was such that not enough horsehide could be obtained, and an updated spec was expedited that permitted the use of steerhide and goatskin. At the end of the jackets' production in 1943, the majority had been made of steerhide, the most readily available leather of the time.

The A2 was not merely a functional garment. It was a status symbol that marked its owner as part of an élite band and it was worn with macho pride. American fighter pilots were not the only ones to wear the jacket during the war. Bomber crews also had them. And, although superseded by another design in 1943, the A2 remained the most popular flying jacket with American airmen throughout the war, in all theaters of operation.

Flamboyant artwork often decorated the fronts and backs of A2 jackets. It frequently replicated the nose art painted on the wearer's aircraft. Pin-up girls of the Vargas variety were popular subjects, and the name of a wife or girlfriend, hometown or state was often displayed. Some designs were suggestive, some lewd. Some carried threats directed at the enemy and a tally of missions already flown. Such decoration, while against army regulations, proliferated and helped to boost aircrew morale.

The jacket art seemed harmless enough until, on November 26, 1943, a B-17 of the 351st Bomb Group was shot down over Germany, its captured crew all wearing A2s bearing the name MURDER INC. With the Nazi propaganda machine anxious to denigrate the Allied "Terror Flieger," such a gift for the Germans was a considerable embarrassment to the Army Air Force. From then on a degree of censorship was imposed on A2 decoration.

Gregory Peck as General Savage in the film *Twelve O'clock High*.

BRIEFING ROOM.
ADMITTANCE BY PASS ONLY.

For airmen of the Royal Air Force there was no equivalent to the A2. The nearest approximation was the sheepskin-lined Irvin flying jacket. The Irvin was a wonderful design, but its bulky form meant that it was never as practical as the A2. Also, King's Regulations forbade the defacing of Air Ministry property by painting on slogans or emblems. Thus, decoration on Irvins does not feature as one of the art forms of World War II and such personalizing was rare. It was common practice among RAF fighter pilots to signal their membership in that élite band by simply leaving the top button of their tunic undone. The practice probably derived from the need for greater comfort and freedom of movement in the cramped fighter cockpit, and to allow scarves to be tucked into the tunic at a time when service dress was still worn for flying duties. A cartoon character of the time, Pilot Officer Prune, provided still another explanation, nonchalantly pointing out that his top button had

been shot off during a dogfight. But the top-button routine was no match for the A2, and more than one RAF pilot managed to acquire one for his personal use.

Today, original and even reproduction A2 jackets are highly sought after. Some purchasers feel that the jacket must be painted, or have a well-worn, distressed look—a used appearance implying the experience of combat.

Walter Konantz of the 338th Fighter Squadron, 55th Fighter Group, recalled the story of his own battle-damaged A2. "On 13th January 1945, I was circling Geibelstadt airdrome, getting ready to strafe it for the second time in a week. I noticed a couple of German planes taxiing, then saw one take off. I watched while he made a climbing one-hundred-eighty-degree turn to the left, passing under me in the opposite direction, I did a tight one-eighty and got in behind him. It was an ME 262 jet and he had not yet accelerated to high speed. We had the new K-14 gunsight installed

a week previously and I had never fired the guns using the new sight in aerial combat. It worked perfectly and I clobbered him with over forty strikes, setting his left engine on fire. He took no evasive action, even after the first hit. He then spiraled into the ground and exploded. Since I still had some ammo left, I picked out a parked plane on the ground and started a strafing pass. Just as I got in range of the parked JU 88, I saw that it was a burned-out hulk from our previous strafing work, so I didn't fire. However, the hornet's nest was stirred up and light flak was coming from everywhere. A single .30 caliber bullet entered my cockpit from the left side, cut a groove in the sleeve of my jacket, and hit the radio control box on the right side of the cockpit. This, of course, disabled my radio and when I climbed up out of there not another P-51 was in sight.

"The weather was lousy and without a radio I hesitated to try going back to England without the help of

Setting a time hack in a briefing session.

In October 1943, these pilots with the 4th Fighter Group at Debden listen intently to the briefing for the mission they are about to fly.

a DF steer, so I found a single P-47, joined up with him and signaled that my radio was out and that I wanted to land with him. He took me to St. Trond, Belgium, where I spent the night and returned to England the next day. Meanwhile, back at the base, my barracks mates had assumed the fiery crash at Geibelstadt was me since they had heard nothing from me on the radio, and were in the process of divvying up my personal belongings as I walked in the door.

"Wish I had that jacket now for a souvenir, but I foolishly turned it in for a new one."

In 1987 the U.S. Air Force decided to reintroduce the A2 jacket in conjunction with the fortieth anniversary of the service. In a climate of severely restricted budgeting, the Air Force requested $7.4 million for the procurement of the new jackets for its pilots. Early in the 1987–88 budget cycle the appropriations committee of the U.S. Senate deleted the proposed funding, some members declaring the purchasing of millions of dollars worth of jackets "expensive and frivolous." The Air Force, however, wanted the jackets in order to help improve the morale of aircrew and perhaps to improve retention in the service. It considered the jacket an excellent means to rekindle the esprit de corps of its front-line flying crews. It lobbied long and hard to retain the jacket-procurement program in the budget and, for a while, it prevailed. Air Force pilots were soon wearing the new A2s. In 1989, however, the House Armed Services Committee deleted funding for the jackets for fiscal 1989 and informed the Air Force that, from then on, each pilot would have to buy his own.

In the end a $5.2 million contract for 53,000 A2 jackets was let to the Cooper Sportswear Manufacturing Company of Newark, New Jersey. It was the largest military contract ever for flight jackets. The Cooper jacket was specified to be in accordance with the Willis & Geiger Style Number A2, the Avirex Style Number 2107G, or equivalent. The first Cooper jackets were delivered to the Air Force in May 1988.

The A2 was worn with pride, never more so than when battle-scarred.

Airmen of the Eighth Air Force relax on base after the day's mission; overleaf: Pilots of the 357th Fighter Group at Leiston re-fly their most recent heavy bomber escort mission.

THE LONG RANGER

A restored P-51D Mustang landing at Duxford, England.

WITH THE ADVENT OF long-range daylight escort missions in mid-summer 1943, the American fighter pilot was severely tested both physically and mentally. Until then the duration of his time in the air on any one European mission had seldom been more than two hours. Now, with the new long-range fuel tanks, the missions would be extended considerably.

Robert Strobell was one of the pilots who regularly flew these demanding missions with the Metfield-based 351st Squadron of the 353rd Fighter Group. He recalled the unpleasant occasion over Germany when pressure from hours of sitting on a hard parachute and dinghy pack dislocated his hip joint. Even the mildest head colds could cause excruciating sinus pain, and the simple need to relieve oneself could bring unbearable discomfort. On another trip, Strobell landed the fighter back in England with his bladder fit to burst. He leapt from the Thunderbolt the instant it rolled to a stop in its revetment and "let go" at the back of the airplane. Looking up, he was face to face with a startled farmer, his wife and children. They could not have known or imagined the four and a half hours of discomfort Strobell had just endured.

For Bob Strobell, and all fighter pilots in the ETO, flak was what worried them most. If the harmless-looking little puffs got you, you were gone. Strobell finally accepted what his commanding officer, Major Glenn Duncan, was telling his pilots. "pay no attention to it. Once it starts, there is nothing you can do about it." Enemy fighters, however, were a different matter. Although, unlike the flak, something *could* be done about them, merely sighting them would "immediately crank up your tension by about five notches. They could be sighted at a great distance as 'bogeys' or 'bandits,'

Pilot John England climbs out of his Mustang fighter, *Nooky Booky IV,* at Leiston, home to the 357th Fighter Group in the Second World War.

bogeys being unidentified aircraft, and bandits enemy aircraft. Seeing them meant that you would close on them to kill or be killed. Believe me, it pumps up your senses in a second."

Over Germany there were other fears too. Strobell remembered: "When you first start flying fighters in combat, you have a tendency to listen to the engine. You watch all the engine gauges—temperature, oil pressure, manifold pressure, and RPMs—rather closely. And you listen. It probably comes from the sobering thought that it might quit over enemy territory. After a few missions, you finally get the message. And that is [that] there is nothing that this watching and listening will do to prevent it if it's going to happen. Suddenly, you are free of this self-imposed tension."

One instrument, though, was watched intently by all pilots during these long-range escort missions—the fuel gauge. Strobell: "Time and distance became a matter of grave concern. Deep penetrations into Germany extended the P-47 to its maximum range. When you were in enemy territory and you knew that you had reached the halfway point of the flight, you started to pray that you would not see or engage enemy fighters. To do so meant opening up the throttle and burning off large amounts of gasoline rapidly in a dogfight, leaving you with not enough fuel to make it back to England. When this occurred, it became a most stressful situation . . . like the time I just made it back to Woodbridge emergency air base and touched down as the engine quit, out of gasoline. At that moment, my wingman went barreling past me on the runway. He'd landed from the opposite direction. That was cutting it too close."

The new, lengthy missions were tough on the American fighter pilots, but they were beginning to pay off. On July 28, 1943, P-47s of the 4th Fighter Group, Debden, routed the Luftwaffe. Equipped with the new long-range fuel tanks, the Americans were protecting the returning B-17s. The Germans were amazed to encounter them over Emmerich on the Dutch-German border, far beyond the P-47's normal range. The Thunderbolts shot down nine ME 109s and Fw 190s, claimed one probable and six damaged, with only one American loss. The 56th Fighter Group, rivals of the 4th, had similar success over the Frankfurt area in early October. As forty twin-engined Messerschmitt ME 110 *Zerstorer* swept in to attack the American bombers, they were surprised by a mass of Thunderbolts bearing down on them. The American fighters were more than three hundred miles from their English base. The heavy, unwieldy Messerschmitts had no chance to lob rockets into the bomber formation, nor were they any match for the P-47s. The German force was decimated, with twenty-one of the ME 110s and eight other fighters being destroyed. Admittedly, there were substantial American bomber losses, but, without their little friends, these would surely have been greater. It was a major blow to the Luftwaffe.

In the latter part of 1943, Thunderbolts provided most of the fighter cover, being capable of a 350-mile radius of action with their extra tanks. It was hoped, however, that the P-38 Lightning would be even more effective with its 450-mile radius. Unfortunately, that was not to be. Despite a fine performance in other theaters of the war, the P-38 was not good enough to turn the tide for the U.S. fighter forces in the European air war. Engine problems

and a poorer-than-anticipated performance against the Luftwaffe limited its effectiveness. Nevertheless, it did have some successes.

Jack Ilfrey flew the P-38 with the 79th Fighter Squadron of the 20th Fighter Group at Kings Cliffe. He became one of the few aces in Europe on this type of aircraft. In his book *Happy Jack's Go-Buggy*, Ilfrey recounted scoring eight confirmed aerial victories, most of them during escort missions. Over Germany on May 24, 1944, he downed two ME 109s, one of them in conventional fashion. The second Messerschmitt collided with Ilfrey's starboard wing, ripping off a five-foot section. He faced the nightmare of a long journey back to base in a crippled airplane over Nazi-occupied territory. He made it back to Kings Cliffe, but his belief that he was "too damned good to get shot down" was badly shaken.

The real success story of the American escort-fighter force was emerging by early 1944. Extending the range of the escorts significantly further, the North American P-51 Mustang surpassed the 450-mile radius of the P-38. With a greater internal fuel capacity, plus external tanks, the Mustang was capable of reaching the Polish border from its East Anglian bases. It was more than a match for any interceptor the Germans could send against the bomber formations and even took on their new jets.

The early Mustangs of the USAAF were assigned to the Ninth Air Force as tactical fighters to support the impending invasion of Europe. But the Eighth Air Force, in its strategic role, was struggling with the escort problem, often sustaining unacceptable attrition in its bomber force. It was quickly realized that these new fighters had been miscast. The 354th Fighter Group (the first American Mustang unit in the UK) was then reassigned from the Ninth to the Eighth for escort work and by December 1943 they were fully operational. General William Kepner, commander of Eighth Air Force Fighter Command, said of the P-51: "It is distinctly the best fighter we can get over here. They are going to be the only satisfactory answer." The Mustang was now arriving in large numbers, making possible the success of the Eighth in Europe. Kepner had been right about it.

As the strength of the Eighth increased dramatically toward the end of 1943, General Arnold signaled a New Year's message to his commanders. "This is a MUST. Destroy the enemy air force wherever you find them, in the air, on the ground and in the factories." The result was BIG WEEK. In February, a massive, unprecedented and sustained assault was unleashed on the German aircraft industry by the Eighth Air Force. More than a thousand bombers took part in

Captain Jack Ilfrey flew P-38s and P-51 Mustangs with the 20th Fighter Group at Kings Cliffe, England, in World War II; left: Another superbly restored Mustang.

a day-by-day pounding of the Reich, escorted now by the new Mustangs, as well as by Thunderbolts and Lightnings. Nearly a thousand fighters protected the bomber force all the way from England to their targets and back again. In their planning, the commanders had projected possible losses of as many as two hundred bombers on the first day alone. The actual figure was twenty-one, thanks largely to the bombers' "little friends." Success at last—overwhelming numbers, improved organization and tactics, coupled with high morale and an outstanding new fighter were, at last, giving Allied air power the edge over the Luftwaffe.

Stepped up in "boxes" and strung out for hundreds of miles, the thousand or so B-17s and B-24s were protected by a similar number of fighters weaving back and forth to keep station with their slower charges. The fighters flew in the Luftwaffe-style "finger-four," the position of each fighter corresponding to the fingertips of an outstretched hand. Other formations of fighters would be sweeping the sky ahead of the main bomber force. Such a massive aerial assembly looked invincible, by this stage in the war, it nearly was. In Big Week alone, the Luftwaffe lost 225 fighter pilots, dead or missing, and 141 wounded—as well as hundreds of new aircraft. Fully one-tenth of their defending fighter force had been destroyed.

The Eighth Air Force now vigorously pursued the assault on Germany. With growing Allied air superiority, the escorts were encouraged to seek out German interceptors aggressively. As one Luftwaffe fighter pilot put it: "No longer was it a case of their bombers having to run the gauntlet of our fighters, but of our having to run the gauntlet of both their bombers and fighters." By

March-April 1944, the Luftwaffe had essentially been defeated—outfought over its own territory. But for the encouragement of the beleaguered German nation, its propaganda machine churned out stories of crippling American losses and glorious German victories. Believing them, one German farmer leveled his old shotgun at a downed Luftwaffe flier, hanging by his parachute from a tree. The rustic was unimpressed by the airman's profanity. "So, the pig of an American Terror-Flieger speaks German, eh?"

Berlin was the next obvious target after Big Week. The Mustang had demonstrated its range and combat capability, and on March 4, 1944, a small force of B-17s, accompanied by twenty Mustangs of the 4th Fighter Group, hit the city. Reichsmarshall Hermann Goering, head of the Luftwaffe, had once boasted that "no enemy plane would ever fly over Reich territory." At the end of the war, when he saw those Mustangs over Berlin, he "knew the game was up."

Sometimes strafing railway locomotives produced spectacular results. On August 2, 1944, a flight of Mustangs from the 364th Fighter Group shot up a train whose wagons happened to contain V-1 flying bomb warheads. The attack occurred near Rémy, France. As the P-51s strafed, the fourth and last aircraft was suddenly enveloped in a huge explosion. The train had vanished, leaving a long row of craters where the wagons had stood. Such was the force of the blast that the other three Mustangs were flung upside down. Above, the remainder of the 364th circled at one thousand feet as top cover. As the blast reached them, every pilot was convinced that his airplane had been hit by flak. Strafing was a dangerous way of earning one's pay.

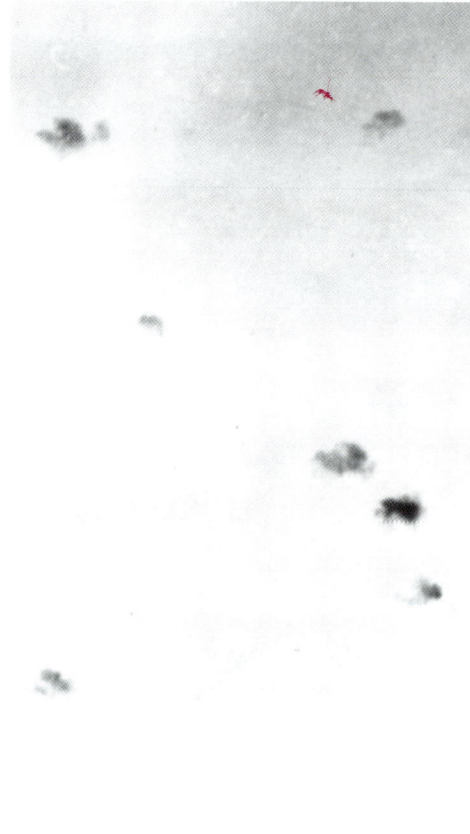

B-17 Flying Fortress bombers of the 390th Bomb Group flying through heavy flak over their German target.

A massive flak tower in the German city of Hamburg.

Trains were fun to hit, but if the American fighter pilot could locate aircraft on the Luftwaffe airfields, all the better. Elwyn Righetti of the 338th Fighter Squadron, 55th Fighter Group, became the top-scoring strafing ace with twenty-seven ground victories to his credit. But it was a form of warfare that was to cost him his life. On April 17, 1945, he crash-landed close to an airfield north of Dresden and was murdered by hostile civilians. Others, too, were brought down by flak during strafing attacks—Beckham, Gabreski, Goodson, Ilfrey, and Godfrey were all taken prisoner. George Preddy, the 352nd Fighter Group ace, was hit and killed by U.S. Army "friendly flak" during low flying. John Godfrey, another of the strafing casualties, had effectively participated in crushing the German fighter force. His capture was a great blow to the 4th Fighter Group. The achievements of individual pilots excited much interest and attention, but it was team effort that really counted in the air. The partnership of Don Gentile and John Godfrey in the efforts of the 4th was a perfect example. Their accomplishments came to the notice of Winston Churchill, who referred to the pair as a latter-day Damon and Pythias. Goering is alleged to have said of these particular "Debden Gangsters" that he would gladly give two of his best squadrons for their capture. A deadly team, they alternated roles as wingman and leader, amassing an impressive score.

RAF fighter pilots had frequently provided withdrawal cover, escorted bombers part of the way out and shepherded stragglers on the way back, but they were never fully integrated into the fighter force of the mass daylight raids by the Eighth. For Johnny Johnson, one of RAF Fighter Command's leading aces, it was a constant frustration: "How we longed for more drop tanks so that some of the many hundreds of Spitfires based in Britain could play their part in the great air battle over Germany instead of being confined to unprofitable sweeps over the familiar but now barren hunting grounds where a man could complete a tour of operations and never fire his guns in anger. We regretted this lack of vision about long-range fighting, for the Spitfire was the best close-in fighter of the lot. With a little foresight the Spitfires could have fought very well in Germany and could have helped the Eighth in its great venture, but it was not to be." This was the American fighter pilot's moment of glory; the RAF fighter pilot had had his during 1940.

It is, perhaps, appropriate that the last word should go to a B-17 tail gunner: "Every time I see a P-51 pilot, I want to go up and shake his hand."

High above us at about 35,000 feet we can see some small specks in groups of four. Each of these tiny dots has a white tail feather. This is the most beautiful sight in the world, because we realize that they are Thunderbolts, our fighter escort. The white plumes are vapor trails. We truck drivers really love these boys. They do a swell job. Their rendezvous with us is right on time. In their groups of four, they skate across the sky, weaving back and forth . . .
—from *Letters From England* by John M. Bennett, Jr.

Don't cheer, boys; the poor devils are dying.
—Captain John W. Philip at the Battle of Santiago, 1898

right: A 56th Fighter Group P-47 Thunderbolt fighter in tight formation with one of the bombers the pilot is protecting; far right: The Lockheed P-38 Lightning, another of the fighter types used by the American Eighth Air Force to escort its heavy bombers on their raids; below: A fine Mustang restoration.

"The Yank racked the 51 around in a steep chandelle, right off the deck, almost reversing course. Two of the other 190s flashed past and pulled up also, but the third was a little further back and turned north, away from the tiger who continued his turn, diving a little now. With the height advantage for the first time, the Yank began firing on a dead pigeon. Smoke immediately trailed from the Fw, but the 51 pilot had to turn away as the other two planes closed in on him. The distressed Fw 190 limped away, trying to get back to Villacoublay, but crashed north of town several miles from the base. Now only two Germans were left, and the American had put a little distance between their planes and his.

"Still on the deck, the Yank was miraculously in the middle. They made a long pass across town while the Mustang closed to a range from which he couldn't miss. The Fw 190 was trying to outrun him this time, but when he saw his nemesis so close behind, the pilot pulled up frantically. The .50s cut loose in a brief, shattering blast. The 190 nosed straight up and its engine died. As the prop windmilled almost to a stop, the plane began to stall about 1,000 to 1,500 feet off the deck, and the pilot bailed out, opening his parachute immediately. It blossomed full and white only a few feet above the trees."
—1st Lt Henry C. Woodrum, a B-26 Marauder pilot with the 344th Bomb Group, Ninth Air Force, describing a dogfight over Paris that he witnessed between an American P-51 Mustang and five Focke Wulf Fw 190s on May 28, 1944

With the end of the war, several P-51s were converted to be flown in air races in America and elsewhere.

THE DECISIVE
STRUGGLE

When the bloom is off the garden, and I'm fighting in the sky, when the lawns and flower beds harden, and when weak birds starve and die, and death-roll will grow longer, eyes will be moist and red; and the more I kill, the longer shall I miss friends who are dead.
—*War* by Flying Officer Nigel Weir

THERE HAD ALREADY BEEN the Battle of France and the air fighting over Dunkirk. But with the Battle of Britain came the most significant and sustained aerial conflict thus far in the war, and both witnesses and participants were left with profound impressions. Pilot Officer Roger Hall was a twenty-three-year-old Spitfire pilot with No 152 Squadron flying from Warmwell in Dorset. He described a typical day's operations during September 1940: "The telephone, that prosaic little household instrument, would become your absolute master and its monotonous ring would harbinger moments of drama to come. The word 'scramble' became the code for emergency take-off at the approach of enemy aircraft, which were known as bandits. An unidentified aircraft was known as a bogey. At this time, most unidentified aircraft coming from the south were German and the majority of takeoffs were scrambles.

"Pull your fingers out, Mandrake. What the bloody hell are you playing at? Get off the air. I can see them, you boys should learn to keep awake, stupid clots. Control had certainly slipped up badly here. We should have been scrambled long before the bomber had got anywhere near the English coast.

" 'Hallo Maida Leader—Mandrake calling—what are your angels now?—over.'

"'Hallo Mandrake—Maida Leader answering—angels two-seven—Maida Leader—over.'

"We were now just starting to make vapor trails and white plumes were streaming away from each of our machines, the vapor from Chumley's aircraft passing over the top of my head in thick, opaque funnels. Vapor trails observed from the air seemed to give the aircraft and those flying them a sort of dignity, serene and splendid. We reached angels three-zero and the CO called up control to advise them. They told us to orbit our position and await further instructions. We began to circle now, on the turn to the south, I could see more vapor trails out to sea and a good deal higher than our own, coming toward us. The CO had seen them too. He called control, giving them the 'Tally-Ho,' and told Maida squadron to start weaving behind and keep a good lookout for those 109s above us.

"Looking into the sun through my fingers, I could just make out the 109s starting to dive. Instinctively my right hand left the control column and operated the transmitter as I shouted, 'Look out, Maida aircraft—109s coming down now at six o'clock above.' I switched over to 'receive' again and Cocky at once led A Flight into a tight turn to port. I stopped weaving, to slide up close behind Chumley and follow. We practically formed a little circle, so tight was the turn, and I could almost feel the nose of Cocky's machine coming up behind my tail and felt more secure because of it. The 109s had certainly picked us out for special treatment, for about eight or nine of them flashed down into the middle of our circle, going straight through it and firing like blue murder as they passed. I wondered if anyone had been hit. It seemed only a few minutes since we had first been

Heinkel HE 111 bombers on a raid against an
English target during the Battle of Britain.

attacked by the 109s, but I had still to fire at something. The bombers had turned south, or should I say, the main body of them had. Quite a number had been shot down by the looks of it and Hurricanes continued to press the rest. I was going toward them, weaving violently as I went, when I saw something that was to change my whole outlook. There was a Hurricane approaching the bombers from the port rear by itself and firing at one of them. The rear gunner was replying with what must have been very accurate fire for suddenly the Hurricane became a mass of flames and the blow could only have been inflicted by the gunner, for there were no enemy fighters in the immediate vicinity.

"I watched the Hurricane turn over on its back and fall away. The pilot himself was on fire as he fell from the machine. As the Hurricane went into a shallow dive, he released his parachute but, as it opened, its shrouds caught fire. The pilot, who had now succeeded in extinguishing the flames on himself, was desperately trying to climb up the shroud lines before they burned through. I witnessed this scene with a hypnotic sort of detachment, not feeling myself able to leave as I circled above. I was thankful to see the flames go out and the parachute behave in a normal manner. I felt a great relief well up inside me, but it was to prove short-lived.

"Two 109s appeared below me coming from the north and traveling very fast toward the south as though they were intent upon getting home safely to France. I disregarded the pilot hanging from the parachute and diverted my attention to the 109s, which appeared to be climbing slowly. I felt I should get my first confirmed aircraft now and turned on my back to dive on them. When I was in the dive I laid my sights well in front of the forward 109 with lots of deflection, for I was coming down upon them vertically. The leading 109 was firing and I looked to see what he was firing at but could see no other aircraft near him. Then I saw it all in a fraction of a second, but a fraction that seemed an eternity. He was firing at the pilot at the end of the parachute and he couldn't possibly miss.

"I saw the tracers and the cannon shells pierce the center of his body, which folded before the impact like a jackknife closing, like a blade of grass that bends toward the blade of the advancing scythe. I was too far away to interfere and now was too late to be of any assistance. If to see red is usually a metaphorical expression,

it became a reality to me at that moment, for the red I could see was that of the pilot's blood as it gushed from all the quarters of his body. I expected to see the lower part of his body fall away to reveal the entrails dangling in midair but by some miracle his body held together. His hands, but a second before clinging to the safety of the shroud lines, were now relaxed and hung limp at his sides. His whole body was limp also, like a man just hanged, the head resting across one shoulder, bloody, scarlet with blood, the hot rich blood of youth that had coursed through his veins for perhaps not more than nineteen or twenty years. It had now completely covered and dyed red an English face

that looked down on but no longer saw its native soil.

"I now noticed black smoke coming away from Chumley's machine and I thought at first his engine was on fire. The smoke was sweeping past my own aircraft and instinctively I looked to see what was behind us, but there was nothing. 'Christ, I'm on fire' was all that came from Chumley as he realized his predicament. He was apparently throttling his engine back, for I could see the blades of his prop slow down and finally stop altogether. I felt a sensation of horror for an instant, expecting to see his machine burst into flames at any moment, and drew back some distance behind him. I seemed unable to say anything to

experience exacted a heavy personal price. As a result of the prolonged mental stresses of combat, he lost his flying category in 1942 and became another "casualty" of the air war.

Sergeant Denis Robinson also flew Spitfires with 152 Squadron and, like Roger Hall, his Battle of Britain experiences left him in continuing wonder at his own survival. The following occurred on August 8, 1940: "The facts are not particularly gratifying for either myself or Pilot Officer Beaumont, who ended up being shot down with me that day. We were returning from a patrol in which we had intercepted the enemy and had used up all our ammunition. We were going back to Warmwell to refuel and re-arm. There were three of us flying in vic formation with Beaumont on the left of the flight leader and myself on the right. We were getting ready for the approach to Warmwell and flying in very tight formation. When I say tight, I mean tight—probably less than a foot from the leader's wingtips. Therefore, Beaumont and I had our concentration firmly fixed on the leader's aircraft. We were preparing to give Warmwell a bit of a show on arrival. Unfortunately, a couple of ME 109s had ideas for a different kind of show. They spotted us and carried out an attack on our unprotected rear, which we had offered them on a plate. We ought to have known better, and did. We knew that it was vital to keep a good lookout at all times, but were lulled into a false sense of security and had relaxed our vigilance briefly. After all, we had had our scrap . . . were nearly safely home and, anyway, we had no ammo.

"The first thing I knew was the thud of bullets hitting my aircraft and a long line of tracer bullets from the attacker streaming out ahead of my

Spitfire. I slammed the stick forward as far as it would go, For a brief second my Spitfire stood on its nose and I was looking straight down at Mother Earth, ten thousand feet below. Thank God my Sutton harness was good and tight. I could feel the straps biting into my flesh as I entered the vertical with airspeed building up alarmingly. I felt fear mounting. Sweating, mouth dry, and near panic. No ammo and an attacker right on my tail. All this happened in seconds, but now the airspeed was nearly off the clock. I simply had to pull out and start looking for the enemy. That's what I did, turning and climbing at the same time. As I opened the throttle fully to assist the climb, I noticed little wisps of white smoke coming from the nose of my fighter. God, no! Fire! Suddenly the engine stopped. Apparently a bullet in the glycol tank had dispersed all the coolant and even the faithful

Merlin could not stand that for long at full power. So that explained the white smoke. Blessed relief. The dread of being burned to death was one of the worst fears. It drew heavily on any reserves of courage one had. You can imagine that by now, my eyes were searching . . . wildly, frantically looking for my adversary—but, as often happens in air combat, not a single plane was to be seen in the sky around me. The release of tension as I realized my good fortune is something that cannot be described. You only know what it feels like to be given back your life if you have been through that experience. The monumental problems that still confronted me, sitting in the cockpit of a battle-damaged Spitfire with an inoperative engine, seemed almost trivial in comparison with my situation of a few seconds before. This experience had a profound effect on me and remains with me to this day.

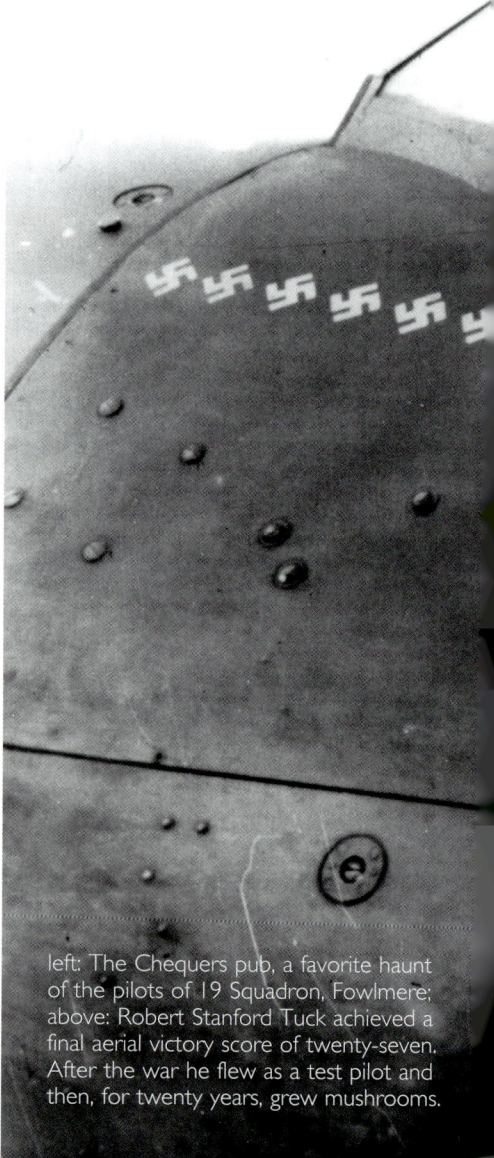

left: The Chequers pub, a favorite haunt of the pilots of 19 Squadron, Fowlmere; above: Robert Stanford Tuck achieved a final aerial victory score of twenty-seven. After the war he flew as a test pilot and then, for twenty years, grew mushrooms.

India
Al Deere
Brian Kingcome
Johnny London
Jamie Rankin
Johnny Kent
Screwball
Beurling
Colin Gray
Bush Bandit
Guy Harris

The signature chalk board from the White H[ar]t pub at Brasted, the pub of choice for B[i]gin Hill pilots during the Battle of Britain; at [left:] Luftwaffe fighter pilots Horst Petzschler, [above] and Werner Mölders, right; at right: A still [fro]m the film *Reach For the Sky* which starred [Ken]neth More as Douglas Bader.

Nothing ever assumed quite the same degree of importance again.

"The end of the episode was something of an anticlimax. I still had plenty of altitude and time to think. I prepared to bail out and began going through the procedure in my mind. Release the Sutton harness, make sure all connections to flying helmet are free, slide the canopy back, roll the aircraft until inverted, push the stick forward and out you go. Then start counting—how many? My memory went blank. Was it three or ten? God! I thought. Well, as long as the interval is sufficient to get clear of the aircraft before pulling the D-ring it should be okay. During this sililoquy I'd got the Spit into a steady glide. It was flying reasonably well and responding to the controls almost normally. I surveyed the damage from the cockpit. Not much, apart from a few bullet holes here and there—particularly in the starboard wing. It seemed a shame to abandon the old bus to certain destruction. After all, she'd served me well and didn't we need aircraft almost as much as pilots? Besides, I was by no means convinced that the bail-out procedure I had rehearsed was not without considerable risk. I could get caught up in the cockpit paraphernalia . . . I might be struck by the tail-plane . . . or what if the parachute didn't open? No. I convinced myself it was too dangerous. I would stay with her and force-land in a suitable field. By now most of the fields looked pretty small, so I decided it would be wheels-up. I picked a field that looked suitable, slid back the canopy, and commenced an approach. At about two hundred feet the boundary loomed up. Full flap and a flare-out near the ground achieved a creditable touch-down. So far so good. I was quite pleased with myself as the Spit slithered across the grass. Then suddenly, I felt her going up onto her nose and, I thought, over onto her back. With an almighty crash the canopy slammed shut over my head and the cockpit filled with dust, completely blinding me. The aircraft seemed to be upside-down and I was trapped. That awful fear of burning returned at full strength. I grabbed the canopy with all my might and threw it backward. To my utter amazement it shot back easily, and the excessive adrenaline-boosted force I had used nearly tore my arms from their sockets. Now I could see that the aircraft had finished up vertically on its nose, in a ditch I hadn't seen from the air.

"My actions now became somewhat comic. It was obvious that I could easily jump clear and I commenced to do so without much hesitation. To my utter horror, I couldn't move. Suddenly, I realized I was struggling against the Sutton harness, still buckled firmly in place. An instant pull released the pin. I was free. As I stood up to jump my head was jerked violently backwards. This time it was my flying helmet still attached to the radio and oxygen sockets in the cockpit. Removing this final impediment I jumped to the ground, leaving my helmet in the cockpit. To my surprise, the Spitfire didn't burn. I stood back and took in the scene as locals arrived to convey me off to a pub in nearby Wareham and fill me with whiskey. I had a slight bullet graze on my left hand but was otherwise unhurt and felt strangely elated. Next day I was back on ops again."

Robinson's survival was probably attributable to two factors. First, his instant reaction of stick hard forward into a vertical dive and the resultant smoke from his engine may have convinced the ME 109 pilot that he had been successful in his attack, or perhaps Robinson had caused the attacker to overshoot his target. Second, ME 109s operating over the Dorset coast far from their French bases were short of fuel and couldn't hang around at length in a dogfight or chase situation. For Denis Robinson, telling his story is a cathartic experience. "In a difficult-to-describe way, it is as though I am speaking for the chaps who did not make it. Their final story would have been infinitely more readable than mine, but telling my tale has helped me to deal with my survival syndrome. One constantly asks: 'Why did I survive . . . why did others not?' "

I do not like the way the cards are shuffled, but yet I like the game and want to play.
—from *Whist* by Eugene F. Ware

Optimism: A cheerful frame of mind that enables a tea kettle to sing though in hot water up to its nose.
—anonymous

Let us, then, be up and doing, with a heart for any fate; still achieving, still pursuing, learn to labor and to wait.
—from *A Psalm of Life* by Henry Wadsworth Longfellow

left: Brendan "Paddy" Finucane was credited with at least twenty-eight aerial victories in his RAF flying career.

A LAST LOOK

Wartime color captured at the Martlesham Heath base of the 356th Fighter Group; right: Fighter pilots relaxing after a mission.

OF THE HALF-MILLION American airmen stationed in England, there must have been many who were thankful to shake its damp soil from their feet at the end of the war. Staff Sergeant Henry Wertz of the Steeple Morden-based 355th Fighter Group expressed their feelings: "Some day to America we'll return, and behind us bridges we will burn, but as sure as there is sadness, joy and bliss, there are some things of England we will miss.

The *Daily Mirror* and its sweetheart 'Jane,' walks in the meadow, through the lane, but when we are back in America once more, to enjoy the things for us there in store, we will soon forget the English way, and settle at home, e'er more to stay!"

Not all the Yanks, though, turned their backs on Britain for good. Some would become eager to come back. American fighter group veterans returned frequently for one last look.

It is said that as men grow older they find more strongly in their hearts the memory of their youth. It is an inexplicable but powerful emotion that draws them back. But coming back can be painful as well as happy. There is sadness at the sight of the cemeteries and wayside memorials. Even those who were not part of the war cannot fail to be moved by the thousands of white memorial markers that stand row upon row beside the Wall of Missing at the Madingley Cemetery near Cambridge. Today it is a place of pilgrimage for returning veterans. Most commemorated here were airmen with the American Eighth and Ninth Air Forces, who died before their time. Those vets who come back have, for the most part, led long and fulfilling lives, and one returning airman confessed to a feeling of guilt as he scanned name after name. "Each of them should and could have been me."

At Steeple Morden the veterans kept coming back, not all of them having "settled at home, e'er more to stay." Their focus has been the imposing 355th Fighter Group memorial at the edge of the abandoned base. It is well kept, in stark contrast to the old airfield around it. Here, weed-choked roadways and perimeter track meander aimlessly among cultivated farmlands and the soil is fertile with the scattered debris of war: a fuel filler cap, a crushed Zippo lighter, a press-stud fastener marked CHICAGO, spent .50 caliber shell casings, and mounds of brick rubble. All are echoes of the past. Casual visitors with only the slightest sense of history realize there is something special about these places. Each crumbling roadway to nowhere is a memory lane, every dilapidated hut a reminder of lost youth. One historian said of these places: "If there are ghosts,

below: A tragic landing accident; top
right: The 357th FG's Jim Browning; other
images are aircraft of the 56th FG.

then they are here."

Decades on and some still come . . . some alone, some in happy, noisy organized groups. Veterans organizations have been the enthusiastic planners of many such parties. The visits have been arranged with military precision and have followed established formats: the airfield and its environs, the "liberty towns" like Cambridge, Ely, and Norwich, the local pubs, the memorials, and, inevitably, the handsome American Cemetery at Madingley. Such was the form of the 361st Fighter Group Association's

1990 UK reunion, culminating in a "48" to London. But advancing years and the presence of wives made this last excursion a more restrained affair than it had been in 1944.

At Bottisham, as at Steeple Morden and so many others, there are memorials to those who flew from the base. At some of the other airfields there are memorials too, but not always in carved stone. Some are much less obvious. At Little Walden, for example, a "state board" was for several decades carefully preserved in the old Ops Block, which had

left: Early P-47Ns were tested in July 1944; below: Bud Mahurin in his Thunderbolt at the 56th FG base in 1943.

become a garage. Nearby, the original control tower was restored to usable condition and became the office of an architect. Many of these airfields, where so much happened, will not be forgotten even though man and nature continue to erase most traces of their past.

It is not only the veterans themselves who have crossed the Atlantic to return to the former bases. Their families and friends have been drawn to these places—people like Gerard Duffy who, as a New York schoolboy, was fascinated by the stories of his older cousin, John Dyer, who had

been a P-38 Lightning pilot with the 20th Fighter Group. Duffy was determined to locate and visit the Kings Cliffe airfield base where it had all happened.

In the 1980s, Duffy was on a study trip to Oxford and took time out to find the airfield. A private pilot, he rented a Cessna and flew over the site, which was pretty much as he had imagined it. The control tower still stood and, viewed from the air, the Kings Cliffe base was still clearly visible. He set up an approach for a landing, as his cousin had done so many times during the war. He passed over the track of the disused runway and decided to return later to explore the place from ground level. As it happened, Duffy was there the very day that the village of Kings Cliffe was holding a garden party to raise funds for a 20th Fighter Group memorial and the villagers welcomed him warmly. Some still remembered his cousin and pointed out Dyer's name and a photo of him in their records of the 55th Fighter Squadron. Duffy was surprised and deeply moved at the interest and affection shown by these strangers who clearly remembered with gratitude the contribution and sacrifices made by some young Americans so long ago.

For both American and British airmen, revisiting their old wartime bases and haunts can be a bittersweet, not always pleasant experience. There can be sadness at the dereliction, vandalism, and change. And some prefer not to go back. For all who do choose to return, though, it is a moving adventure. Eudora Seyfer, wife of a 353rd Fighter Group armorer, George A. Seyfer, accompanied her husband on his return to his old Raydon base. "I am sitting in a bus traveling narrow country roads bordered by green hedgerows. My husband sits beside me. We

During the war and since, air-minded Britain supported many publications relating to the Royal Air Force.

are in the part of England known as East Anglia, mid-morning on a bright Saturday. I am one of fourteen wives on the bus, watching both the scenery and the unfolding drama inside.

"Our husbands, some with thinning gray hair, some with slightly arthritic limbs, several with vials of heart medicine tucked handily in their pockets, lean forward in their seats, peering out the bus windows through the tops of their bifocals—excited and anxious as little boys. Each wears a specially-ordered cap with 353rd FIGHTER GROUP, EIGHTH AIR FORCE printed on the front. They are looking for what's left of Raydon Airfield where they lived for two long, lonesome years during World War II.

" 'I say, it must be near here,' says our travel agent in dignified British English. (His maps of England do not show old World War II airfields.) 'Look!' Suddenly, one of the men points across a flat field toward a bulky, black shadow looming against a blue horizon. 'That's a hangar!' 'That has to be Raydon,' says another with a funny catch.

"Our visit had been carefully planned, even written up in the village newspaper. First we are to stop at the Peabody farm. Mr. Peabody now owns most of the land that was once Raydon airfield. 'Welcome back to Raydon,' Peabody says as he boards the bus. 'As you can see, there is no longer an airfield here, but more of Raydon survives than most World War II airfields. I'd like to show you about.'

"The big bus pulls onto a blacktop road and stops amid a cluster of metal Quonset-type buildings. These are the remaining buildings, now used by the government. And here, too, is the big black hangar.

"The men fan out among the buildings. The three who were pilots head toward the hangar; those who were mechanics, armorers, and radio-men head toward other buildings. I follow my husband, who walks with his friend, Charley Graham, on the remains of the runway. Weeds are growing through the cracks in the old cement. 'Remember when we were standing right here when Colonel Ben's plane crashed?' Charley says.

"Slowly the men drift back toward the bus. I sense a sort of sadness, a letdown. Is this really Raydon? Are these few old buildings in the middle of a farm field all that's left to show for the years spent here? So long ago,

the memories faint. Was it real—that war? Reluctantly, they board the bus.

"Then, from a farm beyond the lane, a woman calls to us. 'Wait, wait!' She runs toward the bus, holding something in her hand. She reaches the group breathless and laughing. 'Forty years ago when you were here, I was a little girl living on my father's farm. One of you hit a baseball over the fence into our farmyard. I found it, but I didn't throw it back. I kept it all these years.' She smiles sheepishly. 'When I heard you were coming, I thought you'd want to see it.'

"The men gather around her, laughing, each holding the old baseball for a moment, then passing it on. Somehow it proves that Raydon was real, the 353rd Fighter Group was here—and that the men were young and vital and strong enough to hit a baseball way over into that farmyard. We thank her and climb back onto the bus. There is a spirit of joy now.

"On to town. Two hundred people live in Raydon. Most of them are here to celebrate the day with us. There are races and games in the schoolyard. Inside, a pot-luck supper is waiting: chicken pies, Cornish pasties, potted shrimp. 'You are the first

Major Urban "Ben" Drew, an ace with the 361st FG, is one of only two men to receive the Air Force Cross for action in the Second World War.

group to come,' they tell us.

"The next morning, we dress in our best clothes. The bus takes us to the tiny Anglican church built in the year 1200 and packed to capacity this Sunday morning. The Americans sit together in the front. When the service ends, Charley Graham stands and asks to say a word. 'We have a gift for you,' He holds the check, our collective gift. 'We have one thousand American dollars to be spent in any way you choose. We ask only one thing: that a little of it be spent for a plaque in this church remembering the men of the 353rd Fighter Group who served at Raydon, so that our children and our grandchildren, when they come to visit, will know that we were here.'

"There is silence in the ancient church; the organ begins to play 'The Star-Spangled Banner.' I look down the rows and see tears on every cheek. How strange life is, I think. An old baseball brought those long-ago days back to life, and a little plaque will keep them living.

"We walk from the cool stone church into the bright morning. We say good-bye and board the bus."

I remember my youth and the feeling that will never come back any more— the feeling that I could last forever, outlast the sea, the earth, and all men. —from *Youth* by Joseph Conrad

Walter Konantz, formerly a Mustang pilot with the 55th Fighter Group: "In the fall of 1944 I was on a weekend pass to London and while window shopping, I happened by a pet shop that had a Scottie puppy in the window. I had left an aging Scottie at home when I joined the Army Air Force in 1943. I went in to look at the puppy and pet it. When the pet shop owner removed the pup and

top left: Tangmere; bottom left: Horham: top
right: Kings Cliffe; below: Bovingdon.

set it on the floor, it wagged its tail and ran over to me in a frenzy of excited greeting. I had no intention of buying the dog but with such a display of 'love at first sight,' I left the pet shop with the pup under my trenchcoat and headed for the train back to Colchester and the 55th Fighter Group. We lived in twelve-man Nissen huts and housebreaking the puppy, now named Lassie II, did have some problems. She eventually learned and became the beloved pet of the whole barracks and was the official mascot of the 338th Fighter Squadron.

"One afternoon I was scheduled for a local test hop in a P-51 and decided to take Lassie for her first airplane ride. There was no place to carry her in the cramped cockpit, so I spread my heavy jacket over the flat surface of the radio just behind the armor plate and set her on the jacket. After takeoff I looked back at her several times and she seemed to be enjoying the flight. When the time came to land, I temporarily forgot about the dog and entered the standard fighter traffic pattern, which was, to fly toward the approach end of the runway at treetop level and, when reaching the end of the runway, breaking upward in a steep left-hand climbing turn to slow up for lowering the landing gear and flaps. Normally, the fighter would pull three or four Gs in the initial hard climbing turn. Immediately after the 'break' I remembered the dog and turned around to look at her. The G forces had her pinned down like a bearskin rug. I eased off on the turn so she could raise her head, and completed the landing. She rode with me in the P-51 on two or three other local flights but she never made a combat mission as we had no canine oxygen masks.

left: Lunch in an air base combat mess; below: Daily routine in a Nissen hut.

"One day while I was on a mission over Germany, someone let her out of the barracks and she headed for my parking area down on the flight line. While crossing the road she was hit by a GI ambulance and badly injured. The ambulance driver, knowing the dog, picked her up and took her to the base hospital. When I landed from the mission and got to the hospital, the Group Flight Surgeon, Captain Randolph Garnett, had me hold her while he took X-rays on the 'people machine'. She had a broken left hind leg near the hip joint. I held her again while he manipulated and set the broken leg. He then wrapped a plaster cast around the leg and middle of her body. We attached an aileron pulley to the end of the leg cast so she could roll the stiff leg on smooth surfaces. After four weeks, we removed the cast and she was good as new.

"Ater finishing my combat tour in February 1945, Lassie and I rode in a B-17 to the staging camp in northern England to begin our journey home. Not knowing what the troop ship captain would think about a dog on board, I gave her two sleeping pills a few hours prior to boarding and smuggled her up the gangplank inside a laundry bag. I kept her hidden under my bunk until we left port in case she was discovered and possibly put ashore. Safely at sea, I brought her up on deck and happily discovered there were three other dogs on board. One belonged to the ship's crew and the other two were 'stowaways.' Lassie spent most of her time on a big hatch cover just aft of the galley. Consequently, the dogs ate real well on steak scraps from the galley.

"When we docked in New York, I repeated the sleeping pill routine and smuggled her off the ship to avoid any possible hassle over customs or quarantine. After Lassie's successful immigration to the U.S., I was released from the Air Force, got married, and started working as a flight instructor at the Nevada, Missouri, Municipal Airport. Lassie went with me every day to the airport and I assumed she would be around the office waiting for me while I was flying. I soon found this not to be true. I had just taken off with a student and happened to look back behind me and there was Lassie pounding down the runway as hard as she could go in pursuit of the departing Cub. When I made a left turn, she made a left turn and was running parallel with the airplane. We circled around for a quick landing and picked up the panting dog and put her in the Cub's open baggage compartment. From then on she always rode in the plane with me while I was instructing students and seemed to enjoy the stalls, spins, occasional loops, and hundreds of landings.

"She logged at least two hundred flying hours there in addition to her military flying time. At this same time I was also in an Air Force Reserve unit at Kansas City flying AT-6s, C-45s, and C-47s. She rode in all those planes several times, once making a flight to Peoria, Illinois, and back on the lap of the AT-6 rear seat passenger.

"Lassie accompanied me and my wife when I was recalled to active duty again in 1951. When we were stationed at George Air Force Base, Victorville, California, in 1953, Lassie's years began to catch up with her and she was in failing health. She got worse and it became necessary to have her put to sleep. Her final flight was aboard a Flying Tiger Air Freight DC-4, her body sealed in a metal box. My parents drove to the Kansas City airport to return her to Lamar to be buried near the other Scottie I had left in 1943."

Primary transport at the Ridgewell base of the 381st BG, bikes lay where they were dropped.

At the end of the war in Europe, much of the American military presence in the UK departed for the United States. Most of the air crews made the journey by troop ship, but many were assigned a bomber to fly back to the U.S. Here, the local villagers turn out to wave good-bye to this B-24 crew who, for a while, were their boys.

YOU Cawn't MISS IT
SERVICE THIS AIRPLANE WITH 100 OCTANE FUEL ONLY

SNAFU

A few of the bombers that the American crews flew on their many raids to Germany.

The Yanks liked to personalize their aircraft; right: One of the airplane storage facilities where the bombers, fighters, trainers and transports were taken for final postwar disposition.

Thousands of American aircraft were disposed of in Europe, but many were brought back to the U.S. where, for the most part, their value lay in the recovery of the aluminum melted into ingot form for reuse in peacetime.

PICTURE CREDITS

Photos credited to the author: PK; to the collection of the author: AC; to the U.S. Air Force: USAF; to the Royal Air Force Museum: RAF Museum; to the U.S. National Archives: NARA; to the Imperial War Museum: IWM.
    P3: *Life* magazine, PP4-5: AC, P6: AC, P7: PK, P9: USAF, PP10-11: John Myers, P12 top: PK, P12 bottom: PK / courtesy Dave Hill, P13: PK, PP14-15 Carlton Smith, PP16-17: USAF, PP18-19: Zdenek Ondracek, PP20-21: Simon Thomas, PP22-23: AC, PP24-25: PK, P27: Vickers, PP28-29: Michael O'Leary, P30 top: courtesy Merle Olmsted, P30 bottom: USAF, P31: PK, PP32-33: San Diego Aerospace Museum, P34 top: AC, bottom: Charles E. Brown, P35: PK, PP36-37: USAF, PP38-39: PK, PP40-41: AC, PP42-43: PK, P43: USAF, P44: PK, P45: PK, PP46-47: USAF, P47: Toni Frissell / Library of Congress, PP48-49: IWM, PP50-51: IWM, P52: USAF, P53: USAF, P54: USAF Museum, P55 both: AC, PP56-57: AC, P58: PK, P59 top: PK, bottom: AC, P60: AC, P63 all: PK, P64 both: AC, P65: AC, P66: AC, P67: AC, PP68-69: USAF, PP70-71: USAF, PP72-73: USAF, P73 bottom: PK, PP74-75: AC, P75: PK, PP76-77: USAF Museum, P77 top: courtesy Lou Christian, bottom: PK, PP78-79: Paramount Pictures, P80: AC, P81: courtesy Andy Saunders, PP82-83: USAF, P84 left: Cuthbert Orde, PP84-85: AC, P85: Cuthbert Orde, P86: PK, PP86-87: AC, PP88-89: all USAF, P89 right: Bundesarchiv, PP90-91: AC, PP92-93: AC, P94 all: PK, P95: courtesy Edith Kup, P96: USAF, P97: De Golyer Library-Southern Methodist University, PP98-99: courtesy Merle Olmsted, PP100-101: AC, P102: courtesy Diana Barnato-Walker, P103 top left: PK, right: PK, bottom: courtesy Diana Barnato-Walker, PP104-105 all: AC, PP106-107: AC, PP108-109 both: AC, PP110-111 all: AC, PP112-113 all: AC, PP114-115: PK, PP116-117: courtesy Monique Agazarian, P118: AC, PP120-121: AC, PP122-123: courtesy Kaz Budzik, P123: PK, PP124-125: USAF Museum, P125: courtesy Nick Kosiuk, PP126-127: AC, PP128-129: USAF, P129: *Life* magazine, P130: Cuthbert Orde, P133: AC, P134, P135, and P136-137: Bundesarchiv, PP138-139: courtesy Oscar Boesch, P140: Bundesarchiv, P142 and 143: Bundesarchiv, PP144-145: De Golyer Library-Southern Methodist University, P147: USAF, PP148-149: USAF, P149: AC, PP150-151: USAF, PP152-153: NARA, PP154-155: De Golyer Library-Southern Methodist University, P156: USAF Academy, P157: PK, P158-159: AC PP160-161 all: De Golyer Library-Southern Methodist University, P162: AC, P163: Zdenek Ondracek, PP164-165: RAF Museum, P166: IWM, P167: both AC, P168: PK, P169: USAF, P170: left: 20th Century Fox, right: AC, P171 left: USAF, right PK, P172 top both: PK / cour-

tesy Greg Parlin, others courtesy Dave Hill, P175: PK / courtesy Dave Hill, PP176-177: NARA, PP178-179: AC, PP180-181: Stephen Fox, PP182-183: courtesy Merle Olmsted, PP184: G. Phelps, P185: courtesy Jack Ilfrey, PP186-187: NARA, PP188-189: IWM, P190 top: USAF, PP190-191: Gary Chambers, P191 top: AC, PP192-193: San Diego Aerospace Museum, PP194-195: Frank Wootton, PP196-197: Bundesarchiv, P198: AC, P199 top: PK, bottom: AC, P200: RAF Museum, PP200-201: IWM, PP202-203: AC, P204: PK, PP204-205: AC, PP206-207: AC, P207 top both: AC, bottom: The Rank Organisation, P208: IWM, PP210-211 all: AC, PP212-213: AC, P214 both: USAF, P215 all: courtesy Merle Olmsted, PP216-217: AC, P217: AC, P218: AC, P219: AC, P220: Toni Frissell / Library of Congress, PP220-221: courtesy Urban Drew, PP222-223: all: PK, PP224-225: AC, P225: AC, PP226-227: USAF, PP228-229: NARA, PP230-231 all: AC, P232: AC, P233: AC, PP234-235: AC, P237: AC.

ACKNOWLEDGMENTS

We are indebted to the following people whose enthusiastic assistance contributed so much to the development and preparation of this book.: Diana Barnato-Walker, Malcolm Bates, Robert Best, Kazimierz Budzik, Gary Eastman, Lou Christian Wilson Fleming, Beryl Green, Stephen Grey, R.C. Harris, Jr, Bill Hess, Dave Hill, Jack Ilfrey, Walter J. Konantz, Edith Kup, Chrystabel Leighton-Porter, Walker M. Mahurin, Eric Marsden, Carroll McColpin, Merle Olmsted, Geoffrey Page, Alan Reeves, Eudora Seyfer, Yanks Air Museum, Chino, California.

Special thanks to the following whose kind help in providing additional photographs, book and article reference material, the loans and gifts of personal memorabilia, interviews, research information, and other forms of assistance aided substantially in the development of this work: Scarlett and Michael Amspaugh, Bailey Brothers and Swinfen Ltd, Paddy Barthropp, Nick Berryman, Tony Bianchi, Len Biggs, Guy Black, Quentin Bland, Keith Braybrook, Stephen Brooks, Harley L. Brown, Anthony C. Chardella, Evelyn Clarke, Jean Hascall Cole, Barbara Darkes, Alan Deere, Peter Dimond, Neville Duke, Chris Ellis, Eddie Ellis-Jones, David Fairbairn, Seymour B. Feldman, Gilly Fielder, Christopher Foxley-Norris, Ella Freire, Royal Frey, James Goodson, James A. Gray, Roger Hall, Pat Hancock, George Hazel, Jack Heath, George Heighington, Mrs J.L Henshaw, Robin Higham, Dave Hill, Robert Hofton, Ralph Hull, Pauline and Ben Jupp, Neal Kaplan, Sally VanWagenen Keil, Richard King, Jimmy Kyle, Robert Loomis, Mike Mathews, Bert McDowell, Tilly McMaster, Len Morgan, Leo Nomis, Michael O'Leary, Peter Osbourne, Bruce

Overstreet, Charles Neville Overton, Richard Paver, Kath Preston, David Price, Jeffrey Quill, Gordon and Winston Ramsey, Jack Raphael. Denis Robinson, Art Roscoe, C.R. Savage, Martin Sheldrick, Anne and Richard Stamp, Ulrich Steinhilper, Robert C. Strobell, Terry Thompson, Denis Todd, Anne and Dickey Turley-George, George Unwin, Marianne Verges, David Wade, Jock Wells, Tim Wells, Frank Wootton, and Hub Zemke.

German Escort: Adapted from *Spitfire on My Tail* by Ulrich Steinhilper and Peter Osborne. Copyright © 1990 Peter Osborne and Ulrich Steinhilper. ISBN 1-872836-00. Available from Independent Books, 3, Leaves Green Crescent, Keston, Bromley, BR2 6DN, England.

The *48 to London* portion of "Time Out of War," by permission of Anthony Chardella, 369th FS Association.

The *Remembering Raydon* portion of "A Last Look" by permission of Eudora Seyfer and *Mature Outlook* magazine.

BIBLIOGRAPHY

Appleby, John T., *Suffolk Summer*, East Anglian Magazine Ltd, 1948.
Barclay, George, *Fighter Pilot*, William Kimber, 1976.
Bergel, Hugh, *Flying Wartime Aircraft, ATA Ferry Pilot*, David and Charles, 1972.
Birch, David, *Rolls-Royce and the Mustang*, Rolls-Royce Heritage Trust, 1987.
Bishop, Edward, *The Guinea Pig Club*, Macmillan & Co. Ltd., 1963.
Black, Adam and Charles, *The WAAF in Action*, London: 1944.
Blake, *Readiness at Dawn*, Victor Gollancz Ltd., 1941.
Brickhill, Paul, *Reach for the Sky: Douglas Bader, His Life Story*, Collins, 1954.
Brookes, A.J., *Fighter Squadron at War*, Ian Allen Ltd., 1980.
Calder, Angus, *The People's War: Britain 1939-45*, Granada, 1969
Cassin-Scott, Jack, *Women at War 1939-45*, Osprey, 1980.
Cole, Jean Hascall, *Women Pilots of World War II* University of Utah Press, 1992
Collier, Richard, *Eagle Day: The Battle of Britain*, E.P. Dutton Co., 1966.
Costello, John, *Love, Sex and War 1939-45*, Pan Books, 1985.
Crook, D.M., *Spitfire Pilot*, Faber & Faber Ltd.
Curtis, Lettice, *The Forgotten Pilot (The ATA)*, Nelson & Saunders, 1971.
Duxford Aviation Society, *Duxford Diary 1942-1945*, 1989.
Fiedler, Arkady, *Squadron 303 (Polish)*, Letchworth Printers Ltd.

Forrester, Larry, *Fly for Your Life: Robert Stanford-Tuck*, Bantam Books, 1973.

Foxley-Norris, Christopher, *A Lighter Shade of Blue*, Ian Allen, 1978.

Freeman, Roger A., *Mighty Eighth War Manual*, Jane's, 1984.

Godfrey, John, *The Look of Eagles*, Random House, 1958.

Goodson, James A., *Tumult in the Clouds*, St. Martin's Press, 1983.

Hall, Grover C., Jr., *1000 Destroyed*, Aero Publishers Inc., 1978.

Hall, Roger, *Clouds of Fear*, Coronet Books, 1975.

Haugland, Vern, *The Eagle Squadrons*, Ziff Davis Flying Books, 1979.

Haugland, Vern, *The Eagle's War*, Jason Aronson, 1982.

Hess, William, *P-47 Thunderbolt at War*, Doubleday & Company, 1976.

Ilfrey, Jack, *Happy Jack's Go-Buggy*, Expostion Press, 1979.

Johnson, J.E., *Wing Leader*, Ballantine Books, 1957

Keil, Sally VanWagenen, *Those Wonderful Women in Their Flying Machines*, Rawson, Wade, 1979.

Kent, J.A., *One of the Few*, William Kimber, 1971.

Kyle, James, *Typhoon Tale*, Biggar & Co., 1989.

Lloyd, Ian, *Rolls-Royce: The Merlin at War*, Macmillan Press, 1978.

Loomis, Robert D., *Great American Fighter Pilots of World War II*, Random House, 1961.

Maurer, Maurer, *Air Force Combat Units of World War II*, Franklin Watts, Inc, 1963.

Miller, Kent D., *Escort: The 356th Fighter Group on Operations Over Europe 1943-1945*, Academy Publishing Corp., 1985.

Neil, T.F., *Spitfire: From the Cockpit*, Ian Allen, 1990.

Nelson, Derek and Parsons, Dave, *Hell-Bent for Leather: The Saga of the A2 and G1 Flight Jackets*, Motorbooks, 1990.

Ogley, Bob, *Biggin on the Bump*, Froglets Publications, 1990.

Nesbitt-Dufort, John, *Scramble: Flying Aircraft of WW2*, Speed and Sports Publications, 1970.

Page, Geoffrey, *Tale of a Guinea Pig*, Corgi Books, 1981.

Peaslee, Budd J., *Heritage of Valor*, J.B. Lippincott Company, 1964.

Polish Air Force Association, *Destiny Can Wait*, William Heinemann Ltd., 1949.

Quill, Jeffrey, *Birth of a Legend: The Spitfire*, London: Quiller Press Ltd, 1986.

Robertson, Bruce, *US Army and Air Force Fighters 1916-61*, Harleyford Pub. Ltd, 1961.

Scutts, Jerry, *Lion in the Sky*, Patrick Stephens, 1987.

Steinhoff, Johannes, *The Final Hours*, The N.A. Pub. Co., 1985.

Sutton, Barry, *Way of a Pilot*, Macmillan, 1942.

Taylor, Eric, *Women Who Went to War 1938-46*, Grafton Books (Collins), 1989.

352nd Fighter Group Association, *The Bluenosed Bastards of Bodney*, 1990.

Townsend, Peter, *The Odds Against Us*, William Morrow & Co., 1987.

Turner, John Frayn, *The Bader Tapes*, The Kensal Press, 1986.

USAF Hist. Studies: No 136, *Development of the Long-Range Escort Fighter*, MA / AH Publishing.

Varian, Horace L., *The Bloody Hundredth, Missions and Memories of a World War II Bomb Group.*

Verges, Marianne, *On Silver Wings*, Ballantine Books, 1991.

Wagner, Ray, *Mustang Designer*, Orion Books, 1990.

Washington Infantry Journal Press, *The 56th Fighter Group in World War II*, Infantry Journal Press, 1948.

Weir, A.N.C., *Verses of a Fighter Pilot*, Faber & Faber, 1941.

Willis, John, *Churchill's Few*, Michael Joseph, 1985.

Wood, Derek, and Dempster, Derek, *The Narrow Margin*, McGraw-Hill Book Company, Inc., 1961.

Woolnough, John H., *Stories of the Eighth*, The 8th Air Force News, 1983.

Wynn, Kenneth G., *Men of the Battle of Britain*, Glidden Books, 1989.

4FG pilots Duane Beeson, left, and Don Gentile.